LOW BEGINNING
Workbook

OXFORD
PICTURE
DICTIONARY

CANADIAN EDITION

OPD

Jane Spigarelli

OXFORD
UNIVERSITY PRESS

70 Wynford Drive, Don Mills, Ontario M3C 1J9
www.oupcanada.com

Oxford University Press is a department of the University of Oxford.

It furthers the University's objective of excellence in research, scholarship, and education by publishing worldwide in

Oxford   New York

Auckland   Cape Town   Dar es Salaam   Hong Kong   Karachi
Kuala Lumpur   Madrid   Melbourne   Mexico City   Nairobi
New Delhi   Shanghai   Taipei   Toronto

With offices in

Argentina   Austria   Brazil   Chile   Czech Republic   France   Greece
Guatemala   Hungary   Italy   Japan   Poland   Portugal   Singapore
South Korea   Switzerland   Thailand   Turkey   Ukraine   Vietnam

Oxford is a trade mark of Oxford University Press
in the UK and in certain other countries

Published in Canada
by Oxford University Press

Library and Archives Canada Cataloguing in Publication
Spigarelli, Jane
  The Oxford picture dictionary, second Canadian edition.
Low beginning workbook / Jane Spigarelli.

ISBN 978-0-19-543351-7

  1. Picture dictionaries, English—Problems, exercises, etc. 2. English language—Textbooks for second language learners. I. Title.

PE1629.S49 2009 Suppl. 1   423'.17   C2009-901411-4

Oxford University Press is committed to our environment. This book is printed on Forest Stewardship Council certified paper, harvested from a responsibly managed forest.

Printed and bound in Canada.

1 2 3 4 – 13 12 11 10

Illustrations by: Argosy Publishing: 71, 92, 96 (top), 98 (top), 100 (top), 113 (pills, cream, tablets, cough medicine, inhaler), 194; Lori Anzalone: 13 (map); Barbara Bastian: 204; Ken Batelman: 155, 223 (top); Fanny Mellet Berry: 121, 165 (top), 256, 292, 295 (top); Arlene Boehm: 51; Kevin Brown: 37, 54, 68, 91, 102, 148, 183, 252; Seb Carmagajevac/Beehive Illustration: 23, 44, 134; Andrea Champlin: 55 (bottom), 242; Mike DiGiorgio: 67 (lower left), 69, 75, 78; Nic DiLauro/Contact Jupiter: 5, 25, 47 (top), 244, 248; Mike Gardner: 7 (top), 33 (top), 39 (top), 49 (top), 71, 97, 112, 132, 164, 171, 197, 227, 230, 255(d); Garth Glazer/AA Reps: 106; Glenn Gustafson: 11 (top), 77, 94, 117 (bottom), 136 (top), 174 (top), 189 (top), 196; Ben Hasler: 93, 56, 59, 179, 219, 250; Betsy Hayes: 135 (bottom); Janos Jantner/Beehive Illustration: 17, 29, 41, 45, 60, 89, 103, 106, 118, 122, 147, 168, 188; Mike Kasun/Munro Campagna: 218; Denis Luzuriaga: 34, 40, 85, 101, 110 (top), 120, 170, 191 (bottom), 241; Chris Lyons/Lindgren & Smith: 191 (top); Scott MacNeill: 18, 66, 70, 79 (top), 86, 87 (chart), 260, 269, 274; Alan Male/Artworks Illustration: 210, 302 (top); Paul Mirocha/ The Wiley Group: 216; Marc Mones/AA Reps: 34, 225, 245; Laurie O'Keefe: 107; Daniel O'Leary/ Illustration Ltd.: 255; Vilma Ortiz Dillon: 259; Chris Pavely: 73 (top), 82, 105 (top), 115 (top), 135 (top), 137, 144, 163, 209 (top), 238, 253; Tony Randazzo/AA Reps: 234; Jon Rogers/AA Reps: 140, 182, 187, 235, 243, 251, 254; Robert Roper/Wilkinson Studios: 2, 8, 32, 58, 65, 83 (top), 87 (top), 104, 119, 136 (bottom), 215; Zina Saunders: 10, 28, 36, 38, 76, 84, 96 (bottom), 99; Marco Schaaf/AA Reps: 61,130, 149, 178, 186, 228 (top), 281; Robert Schoolcraft/Artworks Illustration: 117 (top), 121 (top); Rob Schuster: 13 (chart), 14, 21 (top), 37, 48, 63, 67 (top), 74, 79, 114, 131, 145, 146 (right), 158, 176, 195, 209 (bottom), 213, 226, 237; Ben Shannon/Magnet Art Reps: 3 (top), 22, 42, 62, 81 (top), 91, 98 (bottom), 108, 116, 129 (top), 143, 161, 184, 207, 236, 239; Dan Sharp/The Neis Group: 3 (bottom), 6, 24, 43, 50, 80, 90 (bottom), 95 (top left), 127 (top), 157, 169, 175, 185, 222, 233 (top), 246; Pete Smith/Beehive Illustration: 64, 72, 88, 100 (bottom), 133, 141, 181, 206, 221, 240, 278; Sam Tomasello: 211 (top); Ralph Voltz/Deborah Ltd.: 12, 35, 57, 128, 142, 154, 249,; Philip Williams/Deborah Wolfe Ltd.: 46, 53, 123,126, 153, 177, 208, 224; Craig Zuckerman: 113 (top); dreamstime.com: 262, 270, 282, 283, 288, 297, 299, 300, 303, 307, 308l; istockphoto.com: 264, 286, 289, 293.

Cover Art: CUBE/Illustration Ltd. (hummingbird); 9 Surf Studios (lettering).
Chapter icons: Von Glitschka/Scott Hull Associates

Pronk&Associates: 4, 7 (graph), 9, 20, 21 (chart), 27, 31, 33 (chart), 39 (list), 47 (graph), 49 (crossword), 63 (pie chart), 67 (shopping list), 73 (guide), 79 (graph), 81 (check), 83 (ads), 90 (chart), 95 (receipt), 105 (chart), 109 (crossword), 110 (page), 111, 113 (receipt), 115 (ad), 127 (schedule), 129 (chart), 138, 146 (list), 152, 156 (pie chart), 165 (pay stub), 167 (graph), 172, 173 (crossword), 174, 180, 189 (pie chart), 193, 198, 205, 211 (article), 223 (brochure), 229, 231 (crossword), 233 (graph), 234

Stock Photography: Age FotoStock: 214 (bee), 238 (clarinet, guitar, snare drum, trumpet, violin); Alamy: 52 (mobile home), 150, 159, 162 (flat tire), 166 (cashier), 220 (park ranger), 220 (tour group), 228 (balance beam), 294 (tree), 301 (woman at podium); The Granger Collection: 199 (Alexander Graham Bell, Albert Einstein); Hermera: 55; Historic Tours of America: 220 (ferry); Inmagine: 162 (car on road, people look at map), 166 (shopkeeper); Istockphoto: 30 (older woman), 78 (chicken, cheese, flour), 109 (dental floss, shaving cream, toothpaste), 154 (stop sign, one way sign), 156 (car, truck, SUV), 162 (auto card, policeman), 167 (scissors/comb), 211 (white rose, yellow rose, tulip, sunflower); 212 (shark); 214 (pigeon, feather), 228 (skateboarder), 231 (basketball, shirt, volleyball, baseball, tennis racket, football), 257 (phone), 258 (cake); Jupiterimages Unlimited: 30 (2-year old), 78 (flour), 139 (politician), 176 (hedge clippers, rake, leaf blower), 204 (beach, lake, rainforest), 220 (coral reef), 271 (can of soda), 294 (leaf blower, hedge clippers, rake), 307 (cards, yarn, knitting needles, yarn); National Park Service: 220 (caverns, cave); Northwind Picture Archives: 199 (Marco Polo); PhotoEdit Inc.: 166 (childcare worker); Punchstock: 55 (senior housing, ice cream scooper), 30 (man), 162 (person packing, gas attendent), 166 (auto mechanic), 271 (apples), 301 (graduates); RobertStock: 166 (assemblers); Shutterstock: 15, 30 (infant, teen), 52 (city/night, suburban street, town, townhouses), 55 (soup, steak, chairs), 78 (can, carrots), 95 (woman shopping), 109 (toothbrush, razor), 150 (bicycle, motorcycle, taxi, plane, helicopter), 154 (speed limit sign), 162 (map, Yosemite), 166 (business woman), 167 (computer, hand truck, sewing machine, helmet), 176 (lawnmower, shovel), 214 (spider, butterfly, duck), 216, (wolf, coyote, fox, deer, skunk, bear), 217 (gorilla, elephant, lions, camel), 220 (Grand Canyon, deer), 228 (boxer, golfer, bicycle rider, tennis player), 238 (flute), 247 (arm, toe, heart, face, mouth, toothbrush, doctor, nurse, nose, eye), 257 (cell phone, answering machine, star key, pound key, calling card, cell phone, send button, phone charger, post-it note), 258 (fireworks, flag, turkey, Christmas tree, balloons, book)

Acknowledgements

The publisher and author would like to acknowledge the following individuals for their invaluable feedback during the development of this workbook:

Patricia S. Bell, Lake Technical County ESOL, Eustis, FL

Patricia Castro, Harvest English Institute, Newark, NJ

Druci Diaz, CARIBE Program and TBT, Tampa, FL

Jill Gluck, Hollywood Community Adult School, Los Angeles, CA

Frances Hardenbergh, Southside Programs for Adult and Continuing Ed, Prince George, VA

Mercedes Hern, Tampa, FL

(Katie) Mary C. Hurter, North Harris College, Language and Communication, Houston, TX

Karen Kipke, Antioch Freshman Academy, Antioch, TN

Ivanna Mann-Thrower, Charlotte Mecklenburg Schools, Charlotte, NC

Holley Mayville, Charlotte Mecklenburg Schools, Charlotte, NC

Jonetta Myles, Salem High School, Conyers, GA

Kathleen Reynolds, Albany Park Community Center, Chicago, IL

Jan Salerno, Kennedy-San Fernando CAS, Grenada Hills, CA

Jenni Santamaria, ABC Adult School, Cerritos, CA

Geraldyne Scott, Truman College/ Lakeview Learning Center, Chicago, IL

Sharada Sekar, Antioch Freshman Academy, Antioch, TN

Terry Shearer, Region IV ESC, Houston, TX

Melissa Singler, Cape Fear Community College, Wilmington, NC

Cynthia Wiseman, Wiseman Language Consultants, New York, NY

The author would like to thank:

Stephanie Karras, Executive Publishing Manager, for her collaborative spirit and expert advice in the project's early phases. I am grateful for Stephanie's vision and support throughout.

Sharon Sargent, Managing Editor, for her commitment to meeting the needs of the low-beginning learner, and for her thoughtful critique and vibrant encouragement.

Amy Cooper, editor extraordinaire, for her creativity, insight, and attention to detail, as well as her reassurance and camaraderie.

Marjorie Fuchs and Margaret Bonner, authors of the *High Beginning* and *Low Intermediate Workbooks,* for their inspirational first edition Workbooks.

Bruce Myint, Katie La Storia, and Charlotte Roh for their valuable feedback and problem-solving acumen.

Fran Newman, Image Editor, for her willingness to include me in this integral part of the process, even when it wasn't remotely convenient for her to do so.

Jaclyn Smith and Stacy Merlin, designers, for their artistic creativity and incredible investment of time and energy.

Pronk&Associates for their commitment and skill.

Jayme Adelson-Goldstein, author of the *OPD*, and all around force of nature, for her time, energy, and commitment to this and all the components of the *OPD* program. I am thankful to have had the luxury of her guidance and enthusiasm.

My students and colleagues at Kennedy-San Fernando Community Adult School for the invaluable things they've taught me over the years.

This book is dedicated to my mother, Nora, who listens to me, laughs with me, and encourages me to take many deep breaths.

The publisher would like to thank the following for their permission to reproduce copyrighted material:

pp. 220 (Dalvay-by-the-Sea Hotel): © Copyright 2009, ParksCanada/ J. Butterill/09.93.04.09(27)

pp. 220 (park ranger): © Copyright 2009, Parks Canada/Kevin Bachewich

pp. 220 (tour group): © Copyright 2009, Parks Canada/ P. McCloskey/H.02.18.01.07(02)

To the Teacher

The *Low Beginning*, *High Beginning* and *Low Intermediate Workbooks* that accompany the *Oxford Picture Dictionary* have been designed to provide meaningful and enjoyable practice of the vocabulary that students are learning. These Workbooks supply high-interest context and real information for enrichment and self-expression.

The Workbooks conveniently correspond page-for-page to the 163 topics of the *Oxford Picture Dictionary*. For example, if you are working on page 50 in the Dictionary, the activities for this topic, Apartments, will be found on page 50 in all three Dictionary workbooks.

The *Low Beginning Workbook* addresses the needs of low-beginning learners by practising the most essential, level-appropriate words from the *Oxford Picture Dictionary*. Each topic in this workbook includes a Low Beginning Word List at the top of the page. Here you and your students will find all the words that will be practised on the Workbook page. Word Lists typically provide 9–15 words per topic. Each item in the Word List is reviewed and practised at least twice in the lesson.

All topics in the *Low Beginning Workbook* follow the same easy-to-use format. Exercise 1 introduces students to the target words in the Word List and provides a task designed to review meaning. The tasks in Exercise 1 offer learners opportunities to answer questions about his or her own life, give opinions, or use the *OPD* to personalize the learning process.

Following this activity is at least one content-rich contextualized exercise such as labelling activities, true or false questions, matching or categorizing activities, sequencing tasks, or finding the odd one out. These exercises feature an abundance of art to provide fresh, high-interest context and give essential visual support for the low beginning learner. A variety of graphs, charts, and documents are also provided.

As you peruse this book, you'll notice that about a third of the topics include a Challenge activity as a final exercise. Challenge activities provide higher-level critical thinking practice or additional personalization where appropriate. A standard feature in the *High Beginning* and *Low Intermediate Workbooks*, Challenge activities are introduced here to provide level-appropriate critical-thinking exercises.

At the end of the 12 units is a section called Another Look, a review which allows students to practise vocabulary from various topics of a unit in a game or puzzle-like activity, such as word searches, complete the picture, and P-searches, where students search a picture for items that begin with the letter p. These activities are at the back of the *Low Beginning Workbook* on pages 242–253.

This Workbook includes audio CDs offering one listening exercise for many topics. The CDs give students the opportunity to hear the language of each topic in natural, real-life contexts, including short conversations, narratives, and numeric and spelling dictations. The listening exercises are in the back of the workbook beginning on page 254.

As a teacher in a low beginning classroom, it's always my hope to find material that will motivate and empower my students, as well as make my own life a bit easier. It is my fondest wish that the *Low Beginning Workbook* will help to do that for you and your students.

Jane Spigarelli

Jane Spigarelli

To the Student

The *Oxford Picture Dictionary* has over 4,000 words. This Workbook will help you use these words in your everyday life. Here is some more information about this book:

It's easy to use! The Workbook pages match the pages in your Picture Dictionary. For example, to practise the words on page 23 in your Picture Dictionary, go to page 23 in your Workbook.

It has exercises about real people and things. For example, are you thinking about buying a car? There's a chart showing popular cars on page 156. Do you like shopping for food? Take a look at the grocery list on page 67.

You'll find stories and puzzles in this Workbook and you'll have a chance to give your opinions, too.

There are listening exercises for each topic.

Every unit has a game or puzzle called Another Look. These can be found at the back of the book.

Learning new words is both challenging and fun. I had a lot of fun writing this workbook. I hope you enjoy using it!

Jane Spigarelli

Jane Spigarelli

Table of Contents

4. Food

5. Clothing

6. Health

Contents

10. Areas of Study

11. Plants and Animals

12. Recreation

1. **Check (✓) the things you do and say every day. Look in your dictionary for help.**

   | **Word List: Meeting and Greeting** |
   | **Dictionary pages 2–3** |

   ☐ **Say,** "Hello"   ☐ **Hug**   ☐ **Introduce** a friend

   ☐ **Ask,** "How are you?" ☐ **Wave**   ☐ **Shake** hands

   ☐ **Introduce** yourself   ☐ **Greet** people   ☐ **Kiss**

   ☐ **Smile**   ☐ **Bow**   ☐ **Say,** "Goodbye"

2. **Complete the words. Write the letters.**

   a. _B_ o w

   b. K __ __ s

   c. S __ i l __

   d. G r __ __ t   p e __ p l __

   e. S __ y, "H e __ l __"

   f. S __ a __ e   __ a n __ s

   g. A s __, "H __ w   a __ e   y __ __?"

   h. I n __ r o d __ __ e   __ o u __ s e __ f

3. **Complete the sentences. Use the words in the box.**

   | bow | ~~greet~~ | hug | shake hands |

   a. There are many ways to
   greet people.

   b. People in Japan _____.

   c. People in Canada
   _____ hands.

   d. People in Mexico often _____.

4. Label the picture with the numbers.

1. Smile.
2. Say, "Goodbye."
3. Say, "Hello."
4. Introduce a friend.
5. Introduce yourself.
6. Wave.

5. What about you? Answer the questions.

In my country…

a. I say, "_____" to greet people.

b. I say, "_____" to introduce a friend.

In Canada…

c. I say, "_____" to greet people.

d. I say, "_____" to introduce myself.

3

1. **Check (✓) the words you know. Look in your dictionary. Find the words you don't know.**

> **Word List: Personal Information**
> Dictionary page 4
>
> ☐ **say**   ☐ name   ☐ postal code
> ☐ **spell**   ☐ address   ☐ phone number
> ☐ **print**   ☐ city   ☐ date of birth (DOB)
> ☐ **sign**   ☐ province   ☐ signature

2. **Match the information with the words.**

   _2_ **a.** print   **1.** [J-U-L-I-A]

   ___ **b.** sign   **2.** Julia

   ___ **c.** spell   **3.** [Julia]

   ___ **d.** say   **4.** *Julia*

3. **Complete the form. Use the information in the box.**

| Montreal | ~~Paul Smith~~ | (514) 555-9142 | 212 Central Avenue |
| May 7, 1962 | H5L 1G4 | Quebec | *Paul Smith* |

PERSONAL INFORMATION

NAME: PHONE NUMBER:
   Paul Smith
ADDRESS:

CITY: PROVINCE:

POSTAL CODE:

DATE OF BIRTH:

SIGNATURE:

PERSONAL   OTHER   DIARY

See page 256 for listening practice.

1. **Check (✓) the people and places you see at school every week. Look in your dictionary for help.**

> **Word List: School**
> **Dictionary page 5**
>
> ☐ principal ☐ washrooms ☐ clerk
> ☐ classroom ☐ hallway ☐ cafeteria
> ☐ teacher ☐ main office ☐ computer lab

2. **Cross out the word that doesn't belong.**

   a. hallway   ~~clerk~~   cafeteria   washrooms

   b. cafeteria   computer lab   main office   teacher

   c. clerk   principal   hallway   teacher

   d. washrooms   main office   clerk   principal

   e. cafeteria   classroom   computer lab   hallway

3. **Label the picture with the numbers.**

   1. clerk
   2. ~~teacher~~
   3. classroom
   4. computer lab
   5. main office
   6. hallway

a. 2   b. ___   c. ___   d. ___   e. ___   f. ___

Challenge Write the name of your teacher and the name of the principal at your school.

1. Check (✓) the things you use and the things you do every day. Use your dictionary for help.

Word List: A Classroom
Dictionary pages 6-7

☐ teacher	☐ pencil	☐ **Listen** to a CD
☐ student	☐ pen	☐ **Stand up**
☐ desk	☐ textbook	☐ **Sit down**
☐ chair	☐ workbook	☐ **Open** your book
☐ computer	☐ **Talk** to the teacher	☐ **Close** your book

2. **Match the words.**

_2_ **a.** Talk   **1.** down

___ **b.** Sit   **2.** to the teacher

___ **c.** Close   **3.** your book

___ **d.** Stand   **4.** to a CD

___ **e.** Listen   **5.** up

3. **Label the picture with the numbers.**

1. chair	**3.** desk	**5.** pencil	**7.** textbook
2. ~~computer~~	**4.** pen	**6.** student	**8.** workbook

4. Label the pictures. Use the words in the box.

Talk	Close	Sit	Stand	~~Listen~~	Open

a. ___Listen___ to the teacher.

b. _____ your textbook.

c. _____ to the students.

d. _____ up.

e. _____ down.

f. _____ your workbook.

5. Look at the graph. Answer the questions.

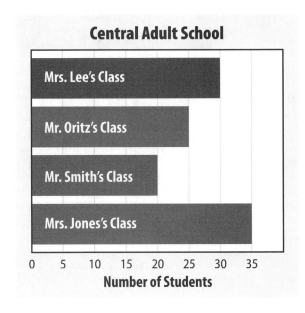

a. How many teachers are there at Central Adult School? ___4___

b. How many students does Mr. Ortiz have? _____

c. How many student books does Mrs. Lee need for all her students? _____

d. How many desks does the school need for teachers and students? _____

See page 257 for listening practice.

1. **Check (✓) the things you do with a pen or pencil. Use your dictionary for help.**

Word List: Studying
Dictionary pages 8-9

☐ **Read** the definition	☐ **Share** a book	☐ **Circle** the answer
☐ **Copy** the word	☐ **Ask** a question	☐ **Match** the items
☐ **Draw** a picture	☐ **Answer** a question	☐ **Take out** a piece of paper
☐ **Work** in a group	☐ **Fill in** the blank	☐ **Put away** your books
☐ **Help** a classmate	☐ **Choose** the correct answer	

2. **Look at the pictures. Check (✓) the correct sentences.**

a.

☐ Put away your books.
☑ Share a book.

b.

☐ Ask a question.
☐ Copy the word.

c.

☐ Draw a picture.
☐ Answer a question.

d.

☐ Choose the answer.
☐ Fill in the blank.

e.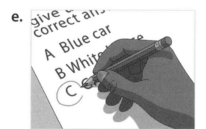

☐ Circle the answer.
☐ Match the items.

f.

☐ Read the definition.
☐ Work in a group.

3. **Unscramble the sentences.**

a. definition. the Read   _Read the definition._

b. your away Put books.   _____

c. classmate. Help a   _____

d. out a paper. piece Take of   _____

e. blank. in the Fill   _____

4. Take the test.

A. Circle the correct words.

1. Help a (classmate) / picture.

2. Read the <u>blank / definition</u>.

3. Choose the correct <u>answer / piece of paper</u>.

B. Copy the words.

1. share _____

2. choose _____

3. ask _____

4. answer _____

C. Match the words.

____ a. Draw   1. the blank.

____ b. Fill in   2. in a group.

____ c. Put away   3. a picture.

____ d. Work   4. your books.

D. Read the story. Circle the words from the Word List on page 8.

I like my English class very much. Every day I work in a group. I share a book with my classmate. We read stories and answer questions together. Then we put away our books and speak English.

5. What about you? Answer the questions. Write *Yes, I do* or *No, I don't*.

a. Do you like to work in a group? _____.

b. Do you share a book every day? _____.

c. Do you ask many questions in class? _____.

d. Do you like to draw pictures? _____.

1. Check (✓) the words you know. Look in your dictionary. Find the words you don't know.

> ### Word List: Succeeding in School
> #### Dictionary page 10
>
> | | | |
> |---|---|---|
> | ☐ **Set** goals | ☐ **Ask** for help | ☐ **Correct** the mistake |
> | ☐ **Take** notes | ☐ **Fill in** the answer | ☐ test booklet |
> | ☐ **Study** at home | ☐ **Check** your work | ☐ answer sheet |

2. Look at the pictures. Put the sentences in order (1–6).

 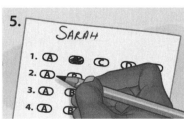 

____ Open your test booklet.

____ Write your name on the answer sheet.

____ Check your work.

____ Ask for help.

_1_ Study at home.

____ Fill in the answers.

3. Complete the story. Use the words in the box.

> | help | home | ~~notes~~ | set | check | correct |
> |---|---|---|---|---|---|

a. I take ___*notes*___ in English class every day.

b. Sometimes I ask for _____ from my teacher.

c. I study at _____ in the evening.

d. I always _____ my work.

e. Then I _____ the mistakes.

f. I like to _____ goals. They help me study.

1. **Check (✓) the things your teacher does every day. Look in your dictionary for help.**

> ### Word List: A Day at School
> #### Dictionary page 11
>
> ☐ **Enter** the room   ☐ **Take** a break   ☐ **Have** a conversation
>
> ☐ **Turn on** the lights   ☐ **Eat**   ☐ **Leave** the room
>
> ☐ **Walk** to class   ☐ **Drink**   ☐ **Turn off** the lights

2. **Read the poster. Write *T* (true) or *F* (false).**

   a. Students cannot eat in the classroom.   _T_

   b. Students can drink water in class.   ____

   c. The teacher turns off all the computers.   ____

   d. Students take a break every day.   ____

   e. Students leave the room to eat and drink.   ____

   f. The rules say to enter the room quietly.   ____

   > **Computer Class Student Rules** 💻
   >
   > 1. Do not eat or drink in class.
   >
   > 2. Turn off your computer every day.
   >
   > 3. Break time is 10:15 – 10:30.
   >
   > 4. Enter and leave the room quietly.

3. **Complete the crossword puzzle.**

   ACROSS

   2. ____ on the computer.

   4. ____ water.

   5. Take a ____.

   DOWN

   1. Have a ____.

   3. ____ to class.

   6. Leave the ____.

1. Check (✓) the things you hear people say every day. Look in your dictionary for help.

> ### Word List: Everyday Conversation
> #### Dictionary pages 12
>
> ☐ **start** a conversation
> *Tell me about . . .*
>
> ☐ **offer** something
> *Here. Use my pen.*
>
> ☐ **thank** someone
> *Thank you very much.*
>
> ☐ **apologize**
> *I'm sorry.*
>
> ☐ **accept** an apology
> *That's OK.*
>
> ☐ **agree**
> *This is a great movie.*
> *Yes, it is.*
>
> ☐ **disagree**
> *This is a bad movie.*
> *No! It's great!*

2. Match the sentences.

_2_ **a.** I'm sorry.

___ **b.** Tell me about your children.

___ **c.** This is a good book.

___ **d.** Here. Use my pencil.

___ **e.** This is a bad movie.

1. Yes, it is.

2. That's okay.

3. No! It's good!

4. They're great.

5. Thank you very much.

3. Label the pictures with the numbers.

a. _2_

b. ___

c. ___

d. ___

e. ___

f. ___

1. accept an apology

2. ~~agree~~

3. apologize

4. disagree

5. start a conversation

6. thank someone

1. Check (✓) the words that describe the weather this week. Look in your dictionary for help.

> **Word List: Weather**
> Dictionary page 13
>
> ☐ hot ☐ cold ☐ raining
> ☐ warm ☐ sunny ☐ snowing
> ☐ cool ☐ cloudy ☐ windy

2. Look at the map. Write *T* (true) or *F* (false).

   a. It's hot in Calgary. <u>T</u>

   b. It's cold in Whitehorse. ___

   c. It's cool in St. John's. ___

   d. It's warm in Montreal. ___

   e. It's snowing in Calgary. ___

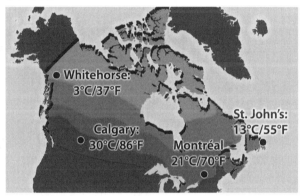

Whitehorse: 3°C/37°F
St. John's: 13°C/55°F
Calgary: 30°C/86°F
Montréal 21°C/70°F

3. Look at the chart. Use the words in the box to describe the weather for each day.

> cloudy   raining   ~~sunny~~   snowing   windy

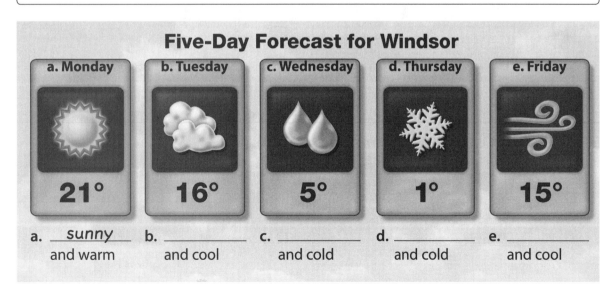

Five-Day Forecast for Windsor

a. Monday	b. Tuesday	c. Wednesday	d. Thursday	e. Friday
21°	16°	5°	1°	15°

a. <u>sunny</u> and warm
b. _____ and cool
c. _____ and cold
d. _____ and cold
e. _____ and cool

Challenge Write three words that describe your favourite weather.

The Telephone

1. **Check (✓) the things you use every day. Look in your dictionary for help.**

Word List: The Telephone
Dictionary page 14

☐ receiver   ☐ cellular phone   ☐ answering machine

☐ key pad   ☐ charger   ☐ voice message

☐ star key   ☐ calling card   ☐ text message

☐ pound key

2. **Label the picture with the numbers.**

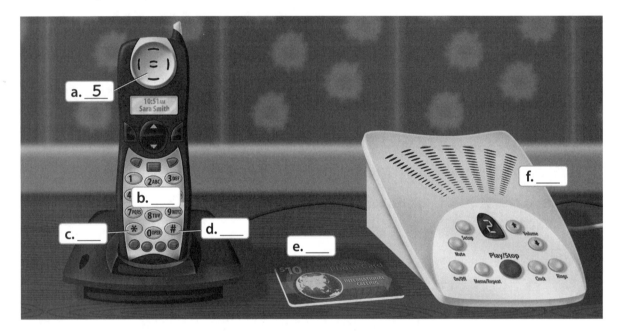

a. _5_
b. ____
c. ____
d. ____
e. ____
f. ____

1. key pad	3. pound key	5. ~~receiver~~
2. answering machine	4. star key	6. calling card

3. **Cross out the word that doesn't belong.**

a. cellular phone	~~answering machine~~	charger
b. answering machine	pound key	star key
c. voice message	text message	telephone
d. receiver	key pad	calling card
e. calling card	key pad	text message

4. Check (✓) the words you know. Look in your dictionary. Find the words you don't know.

> **Word List: The Telephone**
> **Dictionary page 15**
>
> ☐ area code   ☐ **Dial** the phone number
> ☐ phone number   ☐ **Press** "send"
> ☐ local call   ☐ **Talk** on the phone
> ☐ long distance call   ☐ **Hang up**
> ☐ international call   ☐ **Dial** 911

5. **Match the numbers with the words.**

   _3_ **a.** 54-2-555-1931   1. area code

   ___ **b.** (705)   2. long distance call

   ___ **c.** (705) 555-2682   3. international call

   ___ **d.** 1-705-555-2682   4. emergency call

   ___ **e.** 911   5. local call

6. **Tom is making a long distance call. Put the sentences in order (1–4).**

   ___ **a.** Talk on the phone.

   ___ **b.** Hang up.

   _1_ **c.** Dial the area code
          and phone number.

   ___ **d.** Press "send."

1. Write the number next to the word. Use your dictionary for help.

Word List: Numbers
Dictionary page 16

one	_1_	eleven	___	fifty	___
one hundred	___	sixteen	___	twenty-one	___
two	___	twelve	___	forty	___
five	___	eighty	___	sixty	___
nine	___	thirteen	___	four	___
six	___	three	___	seventy	___
eight	___	fifteen	___	thirty	___
fourteen	___	nineteen	___	ninety	___
ten	___	twenty	___	eighteen	___
seventeen	___	seven	___		

2. Study the chart. Complete the sentences. Use the words in the box.

Twenty-five	~~Fifty~~	Seventy-five	One hundred

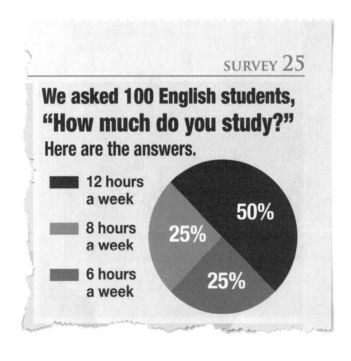

SURVEY 25

We asked 100 English students, "How much do you study?"
Here are the answers.

- 12 hours a week — 50%
- 8 hours a week — 25%
- 6 hours a week — 25%

a. _____ *Fifty* _____
   students study 12 hours.

b. _____
   students study 8 hours.

c. _____
   students study 6 hours or more.

d. _____
   students study 8 hours or more.

Challenge How many hours a week do you study?

 See page 259 for listening practice.

1. Check (✓) the words you know. Look in your dictionary. Find the words you don't know.

> ### Word List: Measurements
> #### Dictionary pages 17
>
> | Fractions | Percents | Measurements |
> |---|---|---|
> | ☐ one whole (1) | ☐ 100 percent (100%) | ☐ inch (in.) |
> | ☐ one half (1/2) | ☐ 50 percent (50%) | ☐ height |
> | ☐ one fourth (1/4) | ☐ 25 percent (25%) | ☐ length |

2. Write *T* (true) or *F* (false).

_T_ **a.** one whole = 100%   ___ **d.** 50 percent + 50 percent = 100%

___ **b.** 50% = one fourth   ___ **e.** one half = 25%

___ **c.** 1/4 = 25 percent   ___ **f.** 1/4 + 1/4 = one whole

3. Look at the picture. Circle the correct words.

a. (Fifty percent)/ Seventy-five percent of the students are men.

b. One fourth / One half of the students are with the teacher.

c. Fifty percent / One hundred percent of the students are at the whiteboard.

d. The length / height of the table is 92 cm.

e. The woman is measuring the length / height of the table.

f. The length of the table is 122 cm / percent.

1. Check (✓) the words you know. Look in your dictionary. Find the words you don't know.

> **Word List: Time**
> **Dictionary page 18**
>
> ☐ hour   ☐ 1:00 (one o'clock)   ☐ morning
> ☐ minutes   ☐ 1:15 (one-fifteen)   ☐ afternoon
> ☐ seconds   ☐ 1:30 (one-thirty)   ☐ evening
> ☐ a.m.   ☐ 1:45 (one-forty-five)   ☐ night
> ☐ p.m.

2. Match the pictures with the times.

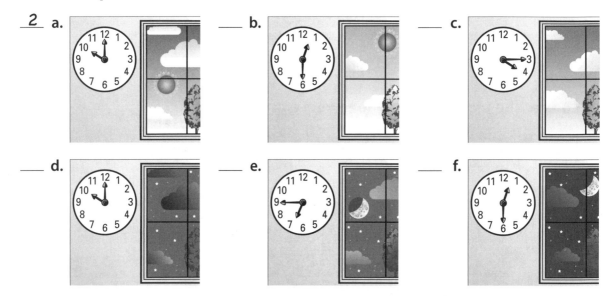

<u>2</u> **a.**   ___ **b.**   ___ **c.**

___ **d.**   ___ **e.**   ___ **f.**

1. It's 12:30 p.m.   **3.** It's 4:15 in the afternoon.   **5.** It's 10:00 at night.

2. It's 10:00 in the morning. **4.** It's 12:30 a.m.   **6.** It's 6:45 in the evening.

3. Complete the sentences. Use the words in the box.

hours	minutes	a.m.	~~seconds~~	p.m.	time

a. There are 60 <u>seconds</u> in a minute.   **d.** What _____ is it?

b. There are 60 _____ in an hour.   **e.** Good morning. It's 7:30 _____.

c. There are 24 _____ in a day.   **f.** It's 10:00 _____. Good night.

4. Check (✓) your time zone. Look in your dictionary for help.

Word List: Time
Dictionary pages 19

☐ early   ☐ Pacific time   ☐ Central time
☐ on time   ☐ Mountain time   ☐ Eastern time
☐ late

5. Unscramble the words.

a. n o m e i t   _o_ n t _i_ _m_ _e_   **d.** t r a l n e C   C __ __ t __ __ l

b. a e l t   l __ t __   **e.** s t e a E n r   E __ __ __ __ __ n

c. l e y a r   e __ __ __ y   **f.** c i f c i P a   P __ __ __ f __ __

6. Label the map. Use the words in the box.

Eastern time   Central time   Mountain time   ~~Pacific time~~

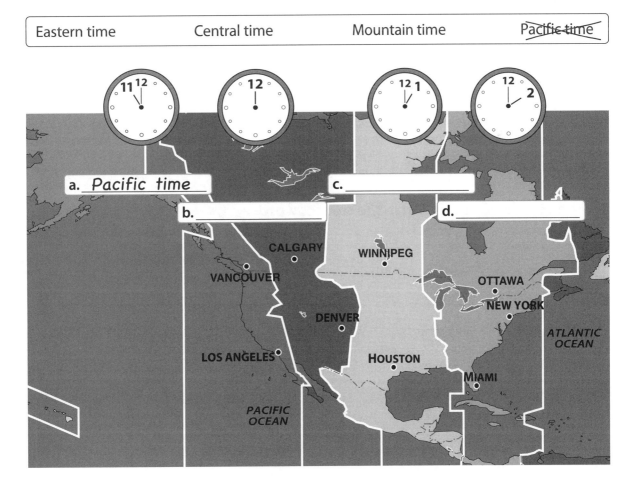

a. _Pacific time_

b. _____

c. _____

d. _____

19

1. **Check (✓) the words you know. Look in your dictionary. Find the words you don't know.**

> ### Word List: The Calendar
> #### Dictionary page 20
>
> | | Days of the Week |
> |---|---|
> | ☐ date | ☐ Sunday |
> | ☐ day | ☐ Monday |
> | ☐ month | ☐ Tuesday |
> | ☐ year | ☐ Wednesday |
> | ☐ today | ☐ Thursday |
> | ☐ tomorrow | ☐ Friday |
> | ☐ yesterday | ☐ Saturday |

2. **Write the days of the week.**

   a. Sun. _____Sunday_____

   b. Mon. _____

   c. Tue. _____

   d. Wed. _____

   e. Thu. _____

   f. Fri. _____

   g. Sat. _____

3. **Look at the calendar. Circle the correct words.**

   a. (Today) / Tomorrow is Sunday.

   b. The day / date today is July 8th, 2012.

   c. The week / year is 2012.

   d. Yesterday / Tomorrow is Monday.

   e. Yesterday was Saturday / Sunday.

   f. The computer class is two days / months every week.

   g. The date / month is July.

   ### July 2012

Sun	Mon	Tue	Wed	Thu	Fri	Sat
1	2	3 computer class	4	5 computer class	6	7
8	9	10 computer class	11	12 computer class	13	14
15	16	17 computer class	18	19 computer class	20	21
22	23	24 computer class	25	26 computer class	27	28
29	30	31 computer class				

4. Write the abbreviation next to the month. Look in your dictionary for help.

> ### Word List: The Calendar
> #### Dictionary page 21
>
> **Months of the Year**
>
> | January | _Jan._ | May | _____ | September | _____ |
> |---|---|---|---|---|---|
> | February | _____ | June | _____ | October | _____ |
> | March | _____ | July | _____ | November | _____ |
> | April | _____ | August | _____ | December | _____ |

5. Complete the chart with the months of the year.

Spring	Summer	Fall	Winter
March	June	September	
April	July	_____	January
May	_____		_____

6. Write the dates.

a. 03/12/01   _March 12, 2001_   d. 07/07/14   _____

b. 09/25/04   _____   e. 02/01/18   _____

c. 05/16/07   _____   f. 06/30/21   _____

7. Look at the chart. Write _T_ (true) or _F_ (false).

a. It's cold in Iqaluit in January.   _T_

b. It's hot in Vancouver in April.   ____

c. It's warm in Ottawa in July.   ____

d. It's cold in Vancouver in October.   ____

e. It's warm in Iqaluit in April.   ____

How's the Weather?				
CITY	Jan.	Apr.	Jul.	Oct.
Vancouver, British Columbia ▶	5°	10°	17°	10°
Iqaluit, Nunavut ▶	−30°	−10°	15°	−7°
Ottawa, Ontario ▶	−11°	6°	20°	7°
St. John's, Newfoundland ▶	−5°	1°	16°	7°

Calendar Events

1. Check (✓) the things you celebrate every year. Look in your dictionary for help.

> **Word List: Calender Events**
> Dictionary page 22
>
> ☐ birthday   ☐ Good Friday   ☐ Remembrance Day
> ☐ appointment   ☐ Boxing Day   ☐ Victoria Day
> ☐ New Year's Day   ☐ Canada Day   ☐ Thanksgiving
> ☐ anniversary   ☐ Labour Day   ☐ Christmas Day

2. Match the holidays with the months.

_3_ **a.** New Year's Day   **1.** November

___ **b.** Victoria Day   **2.** March

___ **c.** Remembrance Day   **3.** January

___ **d.** Labour Day   **4.** December

___ **e.** Good Friday   **5.** May

___ **f.** Christmas Day   **6.** September

3. Label the pictures. Use the words in the box.

> Remembrance Day   Canada Day   ~~birthday~~   New Year's Day   appointment   Thanksgiving

a. _____birthday_____

b. _____

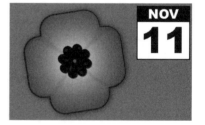

c. _____

d. _____

e. _____

f. _____

22   See page 260 for listening practice.

1. **Check (✓) the words that describe this book. Look in your dictionary for help.**

> **Word List: Describing Things**
> **Dictionary page 23**
>
> ☐ little   ☐ expensive   ☐ easy
> ☐ big   ☐ cheap   ☐ difficult
> ☐ good   ☐ beautiful
> ☐ bad   ☐ ugly

2. **Write the opposite words. Use the words in the box.**

> ~~big~~   bad   difficult   beautiful   expensive

a. little   *big*   d. good _____

b. cheap _____   e. ugly _____

c. easy _____

3. **Look at the picture. Circle the correct words.**

a. The TV is (big)/ little.

b. It's <u>expensive / cheap</u>.

c. The picture is <u>good / bad</u>.

d. They think the TV is <u>ugly / beautiful</u>.

e. It's <u>easy / difficult</u> to see the picture on the TV.

4. **What about you? Answer the questions.**

a. Is your classroom big or little? _____

b. Is your class easy or difficult? _____

c. Do you think homework is good or bad? _____

1. **Check (✓) the colours you see in your classroom. Look in your dictionary for help.**

Word List: Colours
Dictionary pages 24

☐ red   ☐ orange   ☐ pink   ☐ white

☐ yellow   ☐ green   ☐ black   ☐ brown

☐ blue   ☐ purple

2. **Look at the bar graph. Put the colours in order. (Number 1 = their favourite)**

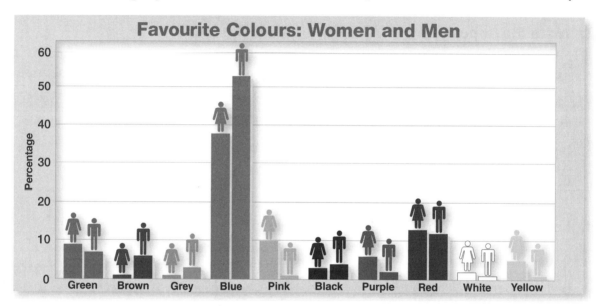

WOMEN'S FAVOURITE COLOURS

1. _____
2. _____
3. _____
4. _____
5. _____
6. _____
7. _____
8. _____
9. _____ and _____

MEN'S FAVOURITE COLOURS

1. _____
2. _____
3. _____
4. _____
5. _____
6. _____
7. _____
8. _____ , _____ and _____

3. **What about you? Put the colours in order. (Number 1 = your favourite)**

___ red   ___ green   ___ purple   ___ light blue   ___ orange

___ yellow   ___ pink   ___ brown   ___ dark blue   ___ beige

Challenge Name 3 colours you see on the front of this workbook.

1. **Check (✓) the words you can use to complete this sentence: "There's a book ____ my desk." Look in your dictionary for help.**

Word List: Prepositions
Dictionary page 25

☐ above   ☐ in front of   ☐ next to

☐ below   ☐ behind   ☐ under

☐ in   ☐ on   ☐ between

2. **Unscramble the words.**

   a. b e d h i n   b _e_ _h_ i _n_ d   **d.** b e w o l   b ___ l o ___

   b. b e n w e e t   b ___ t w ___ ___ n   **e.** t e x n t o   n ___ ___ ___ t ___

   c. u d r e n   u n ___ ___ r   **f.** a v e b o   a ___ o ___ ___

3. **Look at the picture. Write _T_ (true) or _F_ (false).**

   a. There's a book on the table.   _T_

   b. Book A is next to Book B.   ___

   c. The man is sitting in front of the chair.   ___

   d. There's a book under the table.   ___

   e. Book D is above book A.   ___

   f. Book B is between book A and book C.   ___

   g. The table is behind the books.   ___

   h. Book B is below book C.   ___

1. **Check (✓) the money you have with you today. Look in your dictionary for help.**

> ### Word List: Money
> #### Dictionary page 26
>
> ☐ a penny   ☐ a quarter   ☐ ten dollars
>
> ☐ a nickel   ☐ a dollar   ☐ twenty dollars
>
> ☐ a dime   ☐ five dollars   ☐ one hundred dollars

2. **Match the words with the numbers.**

   _5_ **a.** a penny   **1.** 5¢

   ___ **b.** a nickel   **2.** 10¢

   ___ **c.** a dime   **3.** 25¢

   ___ **d.** a quarter   **4.** $10.00

   ___ **e.** a dollar   **5.** 1¢

   ___ **f.** ten dollars   **6.** $1.00

3. **Look at the pictures. How much money do you see? Write the answers.**

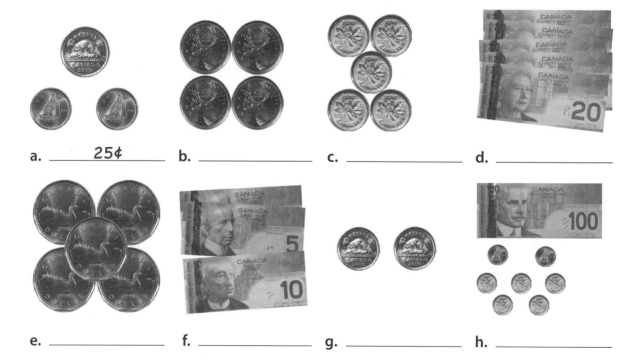

a. _____25¢_____   b. _____   c. _____   d. _____

e. _____   f. _____   g. _____   h. _____

Challenge Look at the pictures in Exercise 3. What is the total of all the money?

 See page 261 for listening practice.

1. **Check (✓) the words you know. Look in your dictionary. Find the words you don't know.**

> ### Word List: Shopping
> #### Dictionary page 27
>
> ☐ **pay** cash   ☐ **write** a cheque   ☐ price
>
> ☐ **use** a credit card   ☐ **buy**   ☐ sales tax
>
> ☐ **use** a debit card   ☐ receipt   ☐ total

2. **Study the receipt. Circle the correct words.**

   a. This is a customer's (receipt) / credit card for Brown's Books.

   b. The <u>total / sales tax</u> is $2.79.

   c. The <u>cheque / price</u> of one English textbook is $19.00.

   d. The <u>tax / total</u> of the receipt is $34.78.

   e. The customer pays with <u>a credit card / cash</u>.

   ```
   --------------------------------------
       BROWN'S  BOOKS
          221 FIRST AVENUE
   --------------------------------------
   ITEM                       PRICE
   1 ENGLISH TEXTBOOK @    $19.00
   1 ENGLISH WORKBOOK @    $12.99

   SUBTOTAL                $31.99
   SALES TAX               $ 2.79
   TOTAL                   $34.78

   PAYMENT METHOD:         CASH
   ```

3. **Study the chart. Complete the sentences. Use the words in the box.**

cash	write	buy	credit	Fifteen	~~pay~~	debit

   a. Thirty-two percent of people like to ___*pay*___ cash.

   b. Thirty-one percent like to use _____ cards.

   c. _____ percent like to _____ cheques.

   d. Many people pay _____ or use debit cards to buy things.

   e. Twenty-one percent like to use _____ cards.

   f. How do you like to _____ things?

   Ways People Buy Things in the Canada

   - 32% cash
   - 15% cheque
   - 31% debit
   - 21% credit

See page 262 for listening practice.   27

1. **Check (✓) the words you know. Look in your dictionary. Find the words you don't know.**

> **Word List: Same and Different**
> **Dictionary pages 28–29**
>
> | | | | |
> |---|---|---|---|
> | ☐ twins | ☐ matching | ☐ navy blue | ☐ **shop** |
> | ☐ sweater | ☐ disappointed | ☐ happy | ☐ **keep** |

2. **Look at the pictures. Write _T_ (true) or _F_ (false).**

   a. Danny is disappointed.   _F_

   b. He likes the sweater.
      He wants to keep it.   ___

   c. Alex is disappointed.   ___

   d. He likes the sweater.   ___

   e. He's happy. He wants
      to keep the sweater.   ___

   f. The boys are twins.   ___

   g. They're shopping with
      their mother.   ___

   h. They're happy.   ___

3. Look at the pictures. Circle the correct words.

a. Mary and Sue Jones are (twins) / disappointed.

b. They're shopping / matching with their mother.

c. Mary likes to match / shop. She's disappointed / happy.

d. Sue isn't happy / disappointed. She wants to go to the park.

e. Mrs. Jones buys happy / matching sweaters for the girls.

f. Then they go to the park. Now everybody is happy / different.

4. What about you? Answer the questions.

a. Do you like to shop? _____

b. What colours do you like? _____

29

1. **Check (✓) the people you see in your class. Look in your dictionary for help.**

    > **Word List: Adults and Children**
    > **Dictionary pages 30–31**
    >
    > ☐ man   ☐ senior citizen   ☐ 6-year-old boy
    > ☐ woman   ☐ infant   ☐ 10-year-old girl
    > ☐ women   ☐ baby   ☐ teenager
    > ☐ men   ☐ toddler

2. **Cross out the word that doesn't belong.**

a. babies	infants	~~man~~
b. 6-year-old boy	woman	baby boy
c. infant	men	women
d. baby girl	senior citizen	toddler
e. woman	baby	man
f. teenager	16-year-old girl	infant

3. **Label the pictures. Use the words in the box.**

    > ~~teenager~~   infant   toddler   senior citizen   6-year-old girl   man

    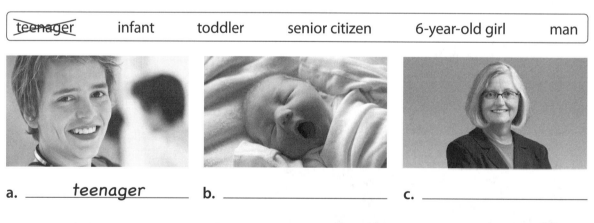

    a. _____teenager_____   b. _____   c. _____

    d. _____   e. _____   f. _____

4. Complete the crossword puzzle.

		²							
¹M	A	N							
							⁵		
				⁴					
	³								
		⁶							

ACROSS

1. John is 40 years old.
   He's a ___.

3. Armando is 16.
   He's a ___.

6. Ivan is 7 years old. Tom is 9.
   They're ___.

DOWN

2. Paulo is six months old.
   He's an ___.

4. Patricia is 74 years old.
   She's a ___ citizen.

5. Amanda is 25. Gloria is 27.
   They're ___.

5. Study the chart. Complete the sentences.

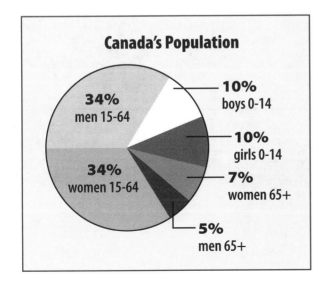

Canada's Population

- 34% men 15-64
- 10% boys 0-14
- 10% girls 0-14
- 7% women 65+
- 34% women 15-64
- 5% men 65+

a. Twenty percent of the population are boys and ___*girls*___ .

b. _____ percent of the population are women ages 15-64.

c. _____ percent of the population are senior citizens.

d. Sixty-eight percent of the population are _____ and _____ 15–64 years old.

31

Describing People

1. Check (✓) the words that describe your friends. Look in your dictionary for help.

> **Word List: Describing People**
> Dictionary page 32
>
> ☐ young   ☐ short   ☐ attractive
> ☐ elderly   ☐ heavy   ☐ cute
> ☐ tall   ☐ thin   ☐ pregnant

2. Unscramble the words.

a. latl   t a _l_ _l_

b. thni   t __ __ n

c. etuc   c __ t __

d. storh   s __ __ __ t

e. ygoun   y __ __ n __

f. veahy   h e __ __ __

g. grepannt   p r __ g __ __ __ t

h. ettraictav   __ t t __ __ __ t __ v __

3. Look at the picture. Read the sentences. Number the people.

1. Carlos is tall and thin. He's elderly.

2. Jim is a young man. He's tall.

3. Nora is attractive. She's with Jim.

4. Mark is with Meg. He's very cute.

5. Meg is a thin, elderly woman.

6. Joanne is pregnant. She is Mark's mother.

See page 263 for listening practice.

1. Check (✓) the words that describe your hair. Look in your dictionary for help.

Word List: Describing Hair
Dictionary page 33

☐ short hair   ☐ curly hair   ☐ black hair

☐ long hair   ☐ grey hair   ☐ blond hair

☐ straight hair   ☐ red hair   ☐ brown hair

2. Complete the sentences. Use the words in the box.

long   ~~straight~~   curly   grey   short   brown

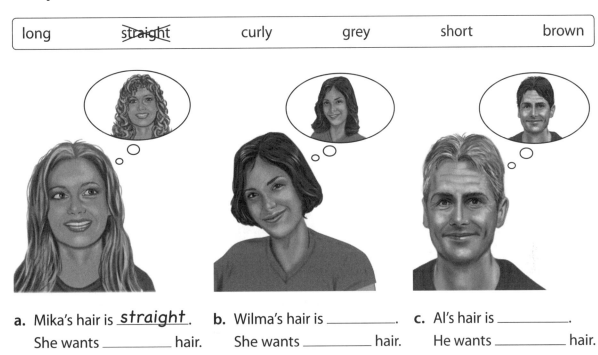

a. Mika's hair is _straight_.
She wants _____ hair.

b. Wilma's hair is _____.
She wants _____ hair.

c. Al's hair is _____.
He wants _____ hair.

3. Look at the graph. Write _T_ (true) or _F_ (false).

a. Eight students have grey hair.   _T_

b. Two students have red hair.   ___

c. Twenty students have black or brown hair.   ___

d. No students have red hair.   ___

e. Seven students have blond hair.   ___

f. Sixteen students have brown hair.   ___

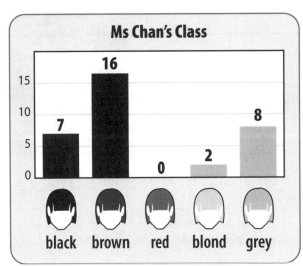

Ms Chan's Class

black   brown   red   blond   grey

33

1. **Check (✓) the people you talk to every week. Look in your dictionary for help.**

> ### Word List: Families
> #### Dictionary pages 34–35
>
> ☐ grandmother   ☐ sister   ☐ wife
>
> ☐ grandfather   ☐ brother   ☐ husband
>
> ☐ parents   ☐ aunt   ☐ children
>
> ☐ mother   ☐ uncle   ☐ daughter
>
> ☐ father   ☐ cousin   ☐ son

2. **Complete the words. Write the letters.**

Men and Boys

a. g r __ __ d __ __ t h __ r

b. f a __ __ e r

c. __ n c l __

d. b r o __ __ e r

e. s __ __

f. __ __ __ b __ __ __

Women and Girls

a. g r _a_ n d _m_ o t _h_ e r

b. m o t h e __

c. a u __ __

d. __ __ s __ e __

e. d __ __ __ __ __ __ r

f. __ i f __

3. **Look at the picture. Circle the correct words.**

a. Sam and Molly are (children)/ brothers.

b. Liz is their sister / mother.

c. Molly is Sam's sister / uncle.

d. Liz and David are children / parents.

e. Sam is David and Liz's cousin /son.

f. David is Molly's father / brother.

4. Read the sentences. Label the people in the picture.

My name is Alicia. My husband is Alfred.

We have two daughters. Their names are Tina and Michelle.

Tina is married to Matt. They have one son. His name is Tony.

Michelle is married to Bill. They have a son named Dan.

Michelle and Bill also have a daughter. Her name is Emily.

a. _____

b. _Alfred_

c. _____

d. _____

e. _____

f. _____

g. _____

h. _____

i. _____

5. Look at the pictures in Exercise 4. Write *T* (true) or *F* (false).

a. Bill is Tina's husband.   _F_

b. Alicia is a grandmother.   ____

c. Tina and Michelle are sisters.   ____

d. Bill and Michelle are parents.   ____

e. Tina and Matt are brother and sister.   ____

f. Tony and Emily are cousins.   ____

Challenge Make a family tree.

See page 264 for listening practice.

Child Care and Parenting

1. Check (✓) five great ways to help a baby sleep. Look in your dictionary for help.

> ### Word List: Child Care and Parenting
> Dictionary page 36
>
> ☐ **hold** ☐ **bathe** ☐ **play** with ☐ **sing** a lullaby
>
> ☐ **feed** ☐ **change** a diaper ☐ **read** to ☐ **kiss** goodnight

2. Look at the pictures. Circle the correct words.

a. Hi. I'm Amir. This is my son, Sam. I (hold)/ bathe Sam and feed / kiss him every morning.

b. I change a diaper / play with Sam.

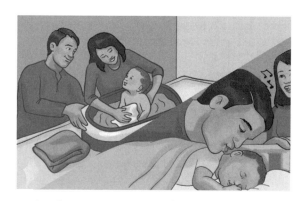

c. In the evening my wife and I bathe / read to Sam. Then we kiss / feed him goodnight.

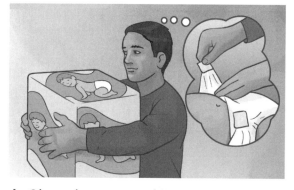

d. Oh, and one more thing! We bathe / change diapers all day and all night.

3. What about you? Answer the questions. Write *Yes, I do* or *No, I don't*.

a. Do you like to play with children? _____

b. Do you like to read to children? _____

c. Do you like to sing to children? _____

4. Check (✓) the things you have in your home. Look in your dictionary for help.

Word List: Child Care and Parenting
Dictionary page 37

☐ bottle ☐ baby food ☐ diaper ☐ baby bag
☐ formula ☐ high chair ☐ wipes ☐ stroller

5. Label the picture. Use the words in the box.

bottles   high chair   diapers   wipes   ~~baby bag~~   stroller

b. _____
c. _____
a. _baby bag_
d. _____
e. _____
f. _____

6. Look at the budget. Answer the questions.

Baby Budget

Item	Formula	[baby food]	[diaper]
Cost per Week	$21.00	$16.00	$9.00

a. How much does baby food cost every month? $64.00

b. How much do diapers cost every month?   _____

c. How much does formula cost every day?   _____

d. How much do formula and diapers cost every week?   _____

e. How much do formula, baby food, and diapers cost every month?   _____

See page 265 for listening practice.

Daily Routines

1. **Check (✓) the things you do every morning. Look in your dictionary for help.**

> **Word List: Daily Routines**
> Dictionary page 37
>
> ☐ **get up** ☐ **get dressed** ☐ **make** lunch ☐ **go** to class
> ☐ **take** a shower ☐ **eat** breakfast ☐ **drive** to work ☐ **work**

2. **Unscramble the sentences.**

   a. We morning. breakfast every eat _We eat breakfast every morning._

   b. She at gets 7:00. up _____

   c. bus school take the every day. We to _____

   d. Joe shower takes every a night. _____

   e. They at make lunch noon. _____

3. **Look at the pictures. Complete the routine. Use the words in the box.**

drive to work	get dressed	eat breakfast	work	~~get up~~	take a shower

My Morning Routine.

	Activity	Time
a.	_get up_	6:00 a.m.
b.	_____	6:15 a.m.
c.	_____	6:30 a.m.
d.	_____	6:45 a.m.
e.	_____	7:00 a.m.
f.	_____	7:30 a.m.

Challenge How long does it take the man to drive to work?

38

4. **Check (✓) the things you do every evening. Look in your dictionary for help.**

> ### Word List: Daily Routines
> #### Dictionary page 39
>
> ☐ **clean** the house   ☐ **come** home   ☐ **read** the paper
>
> ☐ **exercise**   ☐ **have** dinner   ☐ **watch** TV
>
> ☐ **cook** dinner   ☐ **do** homework   ☐ **go** to bed

5. **Look at the pictures. Put the sentences in order (1–6).**

____ They do homework.   ____ They exercise and watch TV.

____ They go to bed.   ____ They have dinner.

____ They clean the house and cook dinner.   _1_ They come home.

6. **Write your evening routine. Look in your dictionary for help.**

My Evening Routine

Activity	Time

See page 266 for listening practice.

Life Events and Documents

1. **Check (✓) the words you know. Look in your dictionary. Find the words you don't know.**

<table>
<tr><td colspan="3" align="center">Word List: Life Events and Documents
Dictionary pages 40–41</td></tr>
<tr>
<td>☐ be born</td>
<td>☐ get married</td>
<td>☐ birth certificate</td>
</tr>
<tr>
<td>☐ start school</td>
<td>☐ have a baby</td>
<td>☐ diploma</td>
</tr>
<tr>
<td>☐ immigrate</td>
<td>☐ buy a home</td>
<td>☐ social insurance number card</td>
</tr>
<tr>
<td>☐ graduate</td>
<td>☐ retire</td>
<td></td>
</tr>
<tr>
<td>☐ get a job</td>
<td>☐ travel</td>
<td>☐ passport</td>
</tr>
<tr>
<td>☐ become a citizen</td>
<td>☐ die</td>
<td></td>
</tr>
</table>

2. **Complete the words. Write the letters.**

   a. g _e_ t a _j_ o _b_

   b. b __ b __ __ __

   c. s t __ __ t s __ __ o o __

   d. b e __ o __ __ __   a c __ __ i __ e n

   e. __ u y a h __ __ __ __

   f. h __ __ e a __ __ __ y

3. **Look at the pictures. Circle the correct words.**

a. Raj and Dhara get /(have) a new baby. The baby needs a <u>birth certificate / diploma</u>.

b. Lin <u>graduates / buys a house</u> today. She's getting her <u>social insurance number card / diploma</u>

c. There's a party for Leticia today. She's going to <u>graduate / retire</u> soon.

d. Frank has a new <u>passport / diploma</u>. Now he can <u>travel / buy a home</u>.

40

4. Label the pictures. Write the numbers.

_4_ a.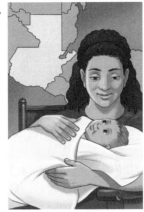

___ b.

___ c.

___ d.

___ e.

___ f.

___ g.

___ h.

___ i.

1. buy a home
2. have a baby
3. graduate
4. ~~be born~~
5. get married
6. become a citizen
7. start school
8. immigrate
9. get a job

5. What about you? Check (✓) three life events that are important to you now.

- [ ] immigrate
- [ ] graduate
- [ ] get a job
- [ ] get married
- [ ] become a citizen
- [ ] have a baby
- [ ] buy a home
- [ ] retire
- [ ] travel

See page 267 for listening practice.

1. Check (✓) how you feel today. Look in your dictionary for help.

> ### Word List: Feelings
> #### Dictionary pages 42–43
>
> | | | | |
> |---|---|---|---|
> | ☐ hot | ☐ uncomfortable | ☐ relieved | ☐ angry |
> | ☐ thirsty | ☐ sick | ☐ sad | ☐ happy |
> | ☐ cold | ☐ worried | ☐ excited | ☐ tired |
> | ☐ hungry | ☐ well | ☐ bored | |

2. Cross out the word that doesn't belong.

a. ~~happy~~   hot   thirsty   d. angry   well   uncomfortable

b. sick   excited   tired   e. bored   tired   relieved

c. happy   excited   cold

3. Look at the pictures. Check (✓) the correct sentences.

a. ✓ She's thirsty.   b. ☐ They're angry.   c. ☐ He's angry.
   ☐ She's bored.   ☐ They're sick.   ☐ He's hungry.

d. ☐ They're worried.   e. ☐ They're excited.   f. ☐ He's sad. She's tired.
   ☐ They're happy.   ☐ They're cold.   ☐ She's tired. He's happy.

4. Look at the picture. Read the sentences. Number the people.

1. Wilma is worried. She thinks her test result is bad.

2. Henry is hungry. He needs lunch.

3. Tran is tired. He worked last night.

4. Raul is relieved. His test result is good.

5. Carol is cold. She needs a sweater.

6. Erica is happy. Her test result is excellent.

5. Read the paragraph. Circle the words that describe feelings.

Today is the first day of English class. How do the students feel? A lot of students are excited about class. Some students are worried about speaking English. Other students are relieved. The class is not too difficult. Many students are happy. They like the teacher. Two students are bored. They need to change levels. Three students are sick. They aren't at school today.

Challenge Write three words that describe your feelings on the first day of class.

See page 268 for listening practice.

A Family Reunion

1. **Check (✓) the words you know. Look in your dictionary. Find the words you don't know.**

> ### Word List: A Family Reunion
> #### Dictionary pages 44–45
>
> ☐ banner ☐ opinion ☐ glad ☐ **laugh**
> ☐ baseball game ☐ balloons ☐ relatives ☐ **misbehave**

2. **Match the words with the pictures.**

<u>5</u> **a.** baseball game ___ **c.** relatives ___ **e.** banner

___ **b.** laugh ___ **d.** misbehave ___ **f.** balloons

1.

2.

3.

4.

5.

6.

3. Look at the pictures. Circle the correct words.

a. The Garcia family is having a (reunion)/ a baseball game.

b. Many of Cesar Garcia's opinions / relatives are here today.

c. Cesar is misbehaving / glad to see his family.

d. His brother and his sister always watch the baseball game / relatives.

e. They have different opinions / reunions about the game.

f. There's a balloon / banner in the living room.

g. The adults laugh / misbehave.

h. The children misbehave / are eating.

i. It's a good balloon / family reunion.

4. What about you? Answer the questions.

Who misbehaves most in your family? What types of things does that person do?

45

1. Check (✓) the things you have at home. Use your dictionary for help.

> ### Word List: The Home
> #### Dictionary pages 46-47
>
> ☐ roof   ☐ floor   ☐ window
>
> ☐ bedroom   ☐ dining area   ☐ living room
>
> ☐ door   ☐ attic   ☐ basement
>
> ☐ bathroom   ☐ kids' bedroom ☐ garage
>
> ☐ kitchen   ☐ baby's room

2. Cross out the word that doesn't belong.

a. kitchen   living room   ~~window~~

b. basement   attic   door

c. dining area   kids' bedroom   baby's room

d. door   living room   window

e. floor   roof   bathroom

f. garage   dining area   kitchen

3. Look at the picture. Circle the correct words.

a. There's a big <u>window</u> in the <u>basement</u> / <u>(living room.)</u>

b. The <u>roof / floor</u> is black.

c. The garage has two <u>doors / floors</u>.

d. There are five <u>floors / windows</u>.

e. The <u>basement / attic</u> has two windows.

4. Label the apartment. Write the numbers.

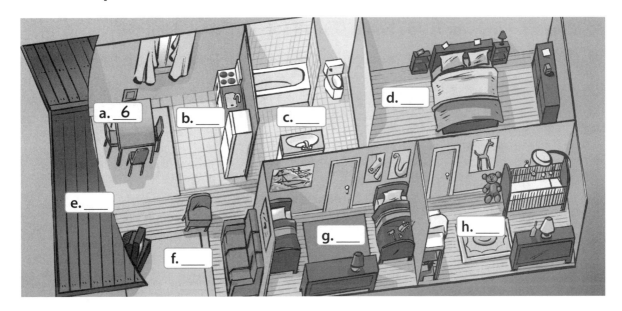

a. _6_ b. ____ c. ____ d. ____ e. ____ f. ____ g. ____ h. ____

1. kids' bedroom   **4.** bathroom   **7.** bedroom

2. living room   **5.** kitchen   **8.** roof

3. baby's room   **6.** ~~dining area~~

5. Study the graph. Mark the sentences *T* (true) or *F* (false).

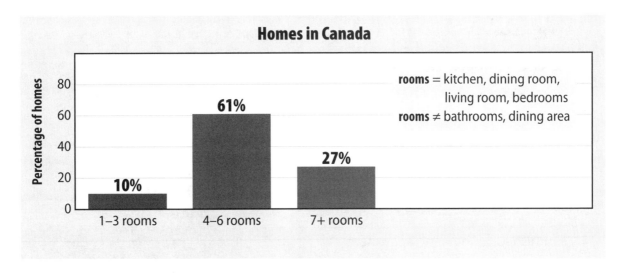

Homes in Canada

Percentage of homes

10% — 1–3 rooms
61% — 4–6 rooms
27% — 7+ rooms

rooms = kitchen, dining room, living room, bedrooms
rooms ≠ bathrooms, dining area

a. Homes with five rooms are popular in Canada.   _T_

b. Fifty percent of homes have three rooms.   ____

c. Ten percent of homes have 1–3 rooms.   ____

d. Seventy-one percent of homes have 1–6 rooms.   ____

Challenge How many rooms are in your home? Name the rooms.

Finding a Home

1. **Check (✓) the words you know. Open your dictionary. Find the words you don't know.**

> **Word List: Finding a Home**
> **Dictionary pages 48-49**
>
> ☐ Internet listing   ☐ **Rent** an apartment   ☐ **Pack**
>
> ☐ classified ad   ☐ **Call** the manager   ☐ **Unpack**
>
> ☐ furnished apartment   ☐ **Submit** an application   ☐ **Paint**
>
> ☐ unfurnished apartment   ☐ **Sign** the rental agreement   ☐ **Meet** the neighbours
>
> ☐ utilities   ☐ **Move in**

2. **Match the words.**

   _5_ **a.** Paint   **1.** ad

   ___ **b.** Submit   **2.** the neighbours

   ___ **c.** Sign   **3.** the rental agreement

   ___ **d.** Meet   **4.** an application

   ___ **e.** unfurnished   **5.** the kitchen

   ___ **f.** classified   **6.** apartment

3. **Unscramble the sentences.**

   a. _She's looking at Internet listings._
   at   She's   listings.   Internet   looking

   b. _____
   furnished.   The   is   apartment

   c. _____
   is   The   kitchen   big.

   d. _____
   The   one   apartment   bedroom.   has

   e. _____
   apartment   This   utilities.   includes

   f. _____
   is   The   month.   rent   a $900

1 bdrm,
1 ba furn apt
Big kit
All util incl
$900 mo

4. Look at the pictures. Put the sentences in order (1–8).

  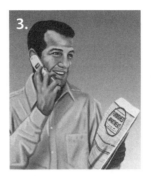 

____ Move in.

____ Sign the rental agreement.

_1_ Look at classified ads.

____ Pack.

____ Submit an application.

____ Find the right apartment.

____ Call the manager.

____ Unpack.

5. Complete the crossword puzzle.

ACROSS

1. ____ an application.

3. ____ the boxes.

5. ____ an apartment.

6. ____ the neighbours.

DOWN

1. ____ the rental agreement.

2. Find the right ____ .

3. Pay for the ____ .

4. ____ the manager.

See page 269 for listening practice.

1. Check (✓) the people and things you see every day. Use your dictionary for help.

> **Word List: Apartments**
> **Dictionary pages 50-51**
>
> ☐ apartment building   ☐ security gate   ☐ landlord
> ☐ elevator   ☐ parking space   ☐ lease
> ☐ stairs   ☐ garbage bin   ☐ smoke detector
> ☐ mailboxes   ☐ emergency exit   ☐ key

2. Cross out the word that doesn't belong.

a. mailbox   key   ~~emergency exit~~

b. elevator   apartment building   stairs

c. security gate   parking space   landlord

d. lease   smoke detector   emergency exit

e. landlord   lease   garbage bin

3. Look at the picture. Complete the sentences. Use the Word List for help.

a. Mr. Topal is the _____*manager*_____.

b. The man is signing a _____.

c. Mr. Topal has the _____.

d. A woman is in the _____.

e. The _____ detector is above the _____.

f. There's a boy on the _____.

4. Look at the pictures. Check (✓) the correct sentences.

a. ☑ The apartment building is on Main Street.

☐ The security gate is on Main Street.

b. ☐ The security gate is open.

☐ The elevator door is open.

c. ☐ There are six smoke detectors.

☐ There are six mailboxes and a smoke detector.

d. ☐ The garbage bin is next to the parking space.

☐ The garbage bin is next to the park.

e. ☐ The vacancy sign is for one year.

☐ The lease is for one year.

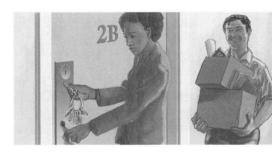

f. ☐ The manager has the key.

☐ The manager has the door chain.

5. What about you? Answer the questions. Write *Yes, it does* or *No, it doesn't*.

a. Does your home have a smoke detector? _____.

b. Does your home have parking spaces? _____.

c. Does your home have stairs? _____.

d. Does your home have a security gate? _____.

See page 270 for listening practice.

1. Check (✓) the places you would like to live. Use your dictionary for help.

> **Word List: Different Places to Live**
> Dictionary page 52
>
> ☐ the city   ☐ the country   ☐ mobile home
>
> ☐ the suburbs   ☐ condo   ☐ senior housing
>
> ☐ a small town ☐ townhouse

2. Match to complete the sentences.

 _5_ **a.** Tan likes his condo because...   **1.** ...they're near the city.

 ____ **b.** We like senior housing because...   **2.** ...there aren't many houses there.

 ____ **c.** Jack likes the city because...   **3.** ...it's busy every minute of the day.

 ____ **d.** Ann likes the country because...   **4.** ...we can talk to other seniors.

 ____ **e.** They like the suburbs because...   **5.** ...it has two parking spaces.

3. Look at the pictures. Circle the correct words.

a. It's a (mobile home)/ townhouse.

b. It's night in the small town / city.

c. They like their home in the suburbs / country.

d. Rayville is a big city / small town.

e. Kristy's townhouse / mobile home is in the city.

f. This senior housing / suburb is very popular.

1. Check (✓) the things you see outside every day. Use your dictionary for help.

Word List: A House and Yard
Dictionary page 53

☐ mailbox   ☐ patio   ☐ sprinkler

☐ driveway   ☐ flower bed   ☐ garbage can

☐ front door ☐ hose   ☐ lawn

2. Complete the words. Write the letters.

a. d _r_ i _v_ e w _a_ y

b. p a t __ __

c. __ o s __

d. l __ __ n

e. m __ __ l b __ __

f. f l __ __ __ r __ e __

3. Label the picture. Use the words in the box.

flower bed   ~~front door~~   garbage can   hose   lawn   sprinkler

a. front door

b. _____

c. _____

d. _____

e. _____

f. _____

A Kitchen

1. Check (✓) the things you use every week. Use your dictionary for help.

☐ sink	☐ freezer	☐ stove
☐ dishwasher	☐ microwave	☐ oven
☐ refrigerator	☐ pot	☐ pan

2. Cross out the word that doesn't belong.

a. sink   dishwasher   ~~microwave~~

b. oven   stove   refrigerator

c. freezer   oven   refrigerator

d. pan   pot   freezer

e. sink   oven   microwave

3. What's wrong with the picture? Circle the correct words.

a. The (refrigerator)/ freezer door is open.

b. The oven / dishwasher doesn't have a door.

c. The toaster / refrigerator is below the microwave.

d. There's too much water in the dishwasher / sink.

e. The pot / pan is on the floor.

f. The pot / pan is too hot.

1. Check (✓) the things you use every morning. Use your dictionary for help.

> **Word List: A Dining Area**
> Dictionary page 55
>
> ☐ plate   ☐ knife   ☐ dining room chair
> ☐ bowl   ☐ spoon   ☐ dining room table
> ☐ fork   ☐ coffee mug   ☐ napkin

2. What do they need? Match the words with the pictures.

_2_ **a.** coffee mug

___ **b.** napkin

___ **c.** bowl and spoon

___ **d.** knife and fork

___ **e.** table

___ **f.** spoon

1.
2.
3.
4.
5.
6.

3. Look at the picture. Write the numbers.

1. ~~fork~~
2. chair
3. knife
4. plate
5. spoon
6. table
7. napkin

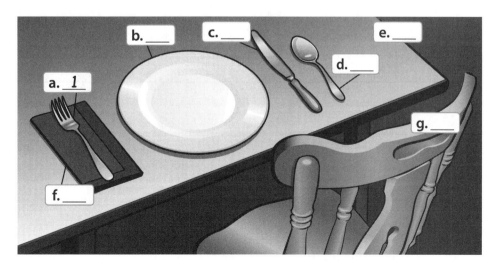

Challenge Which two things from the Word List are NOT in the picture?

1. Check (✓) the things people turn on and off. Use your dictionary for help.

Word List: A Living Room
Dictionary page 56

☐ TV   ☐ fireplace   ☐ coffee table
☐ DVD player   ☐ floor lamp   ☐ armchair
☐ stereo system   ☐ sofa   ☐ carpet

2. Unscramble the words.

a. fosa   s _o_ f _a_

b. cerpat   c a __ p __ __

c. amrchiar   __ r m __ h __ __ r

d. ficreplae   f __ __ __ p l __ __ __

e. roofl lapm   f l __ __ __   l __ __ p

f. feecof atble   c __ f f __ __   t __ b __ __

3. Read the directions. Complete the picture.

a. Draw a stereo system on the table next to the sofa.

b. Draw an armchair next to the fireplace.

c. Draw a TV above the DVD player.

d. Draw a floor lamp next to the sofa.

e. Draw a coffee table in front of the sofa.

    See page 271 for listening practice.

1. **Check (✓) the things that use water. Use your dictionary for help.**

> ### Word List: A Bathroom
> #### Dictionary page 57
>
> ☐ bathtub   ☐ shower curtain   ☐ toilet paper
>
> ☐ soap   ☐ towel   ☐ toilet
>
> ☐ shower   ☐ mirror   ☐ sink

2. **Complete the words. Write the letters.**

a. s h _o_ w _e_ r

b. ___ i ___ k

c. m i ___ ___ o r

d. s ___ ___ p

e. ___ o ___ l ___ t

f. ___ o ___ ___ l

g. b ___ t ___ t ___ ___

h. t ___ ___ l ___ t p ___ p ___ ___

3. **Look at the pictures. Write the numbers.**

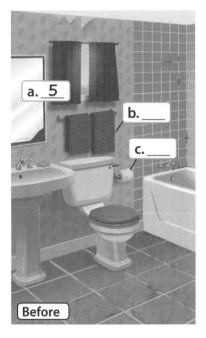

a. 5
b. ___
c. ___

Before

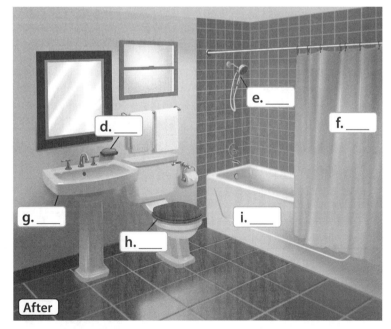

d. ___
e. ___
f. ___
g. ___
h. ___
i. ___

After

1. toilet

2. towels

3. shower curtain

4. bathtub

5. ~~mirror~~

6. soap

7. shower

8. sink

9. toilet paper

Challenge Name the things in the "after" picture that are new.

A Bedroom

1. **Check (✓) the things in your bedroom. Use your dictionary for help.**

> **Word List: A Bedroom**
> **Dictionary page 58**
>
> ☐ dresser   ☐ bed   ☐ blanket
>
> ☐ closet   ☐ pillow   ☐ night table
>
> ☐ curtains   ☐ sheet   ☐ lamp

2. **Look at the picture in Exercise 3. Match the words with the sentences.**

   _2_ **a.** clothes   **1.** They're on the windows.

   ___ **b.** sheets   **2.** They're in the closet.

   ___ **c.** curtains   **3.** It's on the bed.

   ___ **d.** lamp   **4.** It's next to the bed.

   ___ **e.** night table   **5.** They're on the bed.

   ___ **f.** pillow   **6.** It's on the night table.

3. **Look at the picture. Circle the correct words.**

   a. The (blanket)/ pillow is on the floor.

   b. There's a towel on the night table / bed.

   c. There's a phone and a lamp / sheet on the night table.

   d. The night table / closet is open.

   e. There are some clothes on the dresser / blanket.

   f. The night table / curtains are pink.

   g. The girl is in the bed / closet.

   h. She's sleeping on a blanket / pillow.

1. Check (✓) the kids' bedroom furniture. Use your dictionary for help.

Word List: The Kids' Bedroom
Dictionary page 59

☐ changing table   ☐ baby monitor   ☐ toy chest

☐ crib   ☐ bunk beds   ☐ blocks

☐ chest of drawers   ☐ ball   ☐ doll

2. Cross out the word that doesn't belong.

a. ~~toy chest~~   bunk beds   crib

b. crib   kids' bedroom   changing table

c. blocks   changing table   ball

d. toy   blocks   chest of drawers

e. ball   doll   bunk beds

3. Read the sentences. Complete the picture.

a. Draw a doll on the changing table.

b. Draw a baby monitor on the chest of drawers.

c. Draw a toy chest next to the crib.

d. Draw some blocks on the bunk beds.

e. Draw a ball on the toy chest.

f. Draw a toy on the chest of drawers.

Housework

1. **Check (✓) the things you do every week. Use your dictionary for help.**

Dictionary page 60

☐ **dust** the furniture   ☐ **make** the bed   ☐ **sweep** the floor

☐ **clean** the oven   ☐ **vacuum** the carpet   ☐ **wash** the dishes

☐ **mop** the floor   ☐ **wash** the windows   ☐ **take out** the garbage

2. **Match the words.**

_4_ **a.** wash   **1.** the furniture

___ **b.** make   **2.** the garbage

___ **c.** dust   **3.** the carpet

___ **d.** mop   **4.** the windows

___ **e.** vacuum   **5.** the floor

___ **f.** take out   **6.** the bed

3. **Look at the picture. Read the sentences. Number the people.**

1. Jim vacuums the carpet.   3. Paul takes out the trash.   5. Lian sweeps the floor.
2. Wen washes the windows.   4. Mira cleans the oven.   6. Hua washes the dishes.

See page 272 for listening practice.

Cleaning Supplies

1. **Check (✓) the things you have at home. Use your dictionary for help.**

Word List: Cleaning Supplies
Dictionary page 61

☐ rubber gloves   ☐ rags   ☐ broom
☐ mop   ☐ vacuum cleaner   ☐ dish towel
☐ bucket   ☐ glass cleaner   ☐ trash bags

2. **Match the sentences with the words.**

__6__ **a.** I have to clean the oven.   **1.** vacuum cleaner

____ **b.** I have to mop the floor.   **2.** broom

____ **c.** She wants to sweep the floor.   **3.** glass cleaner and rags

____ **d.** Please help me with the dishes.   **4.** trash bag

____ **e.** They want to wash the windows.   **5.** dish towel

____ **f.** He's taking out the garbage.   **6.** rubber gloves

____ **g.** I want to vacuum the carpet.   **7.** bucket and a mop

3. **Label the cleaning supplies. Write the numbers.**

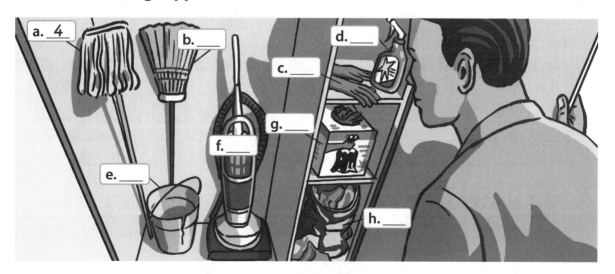

a. 4   b. ___   d. ___   c. ___   g. ___   f. ___   e. ___   h. ___

1. broom   **3.** glass cleaner   **5.** rags   **7.** garbage bags
2. bucket   **4.** mop   **6.** rubber gloves   **8.** vacuum

Challenge Look at the picture. What does Sam need to buy?

1. Check (✓) the words and phrases you know. Open your dictionary. Find the words you don't know.

> ### Word List: Household Problems and Repairs
> #### Dictionary page 62
>
> | | | |
> |---|---|---|
> | ☐ The water heater is **not working** | ☐ The window is **broken** | ☐ electrician |
> | ☐ The power is **out** | ☐ The lock is **broken** | ☐ repair person |
> | ☐ The roof is **leaking** | ☐ roofer | ☐ locksmith |

2. Unscramble the sentences.

a. The broken. is lock   _The lock is broken._

b. is power The out.   _____

c. roof The leaking. is   _____

d. broken. is window The   _____

e. heater isn't The water working.   _____

3. Look at the pictures. Check (✓) the correct sentences.

a. ✓ She's calling a roofer.

☐ The power is out.

b. ☐ The water heater is leaking.

☐ He needs a locksmith.

c. ☐ He's a repair person.

☐ He's looking for an electrician.

d. ☐ He needs an electrician.

☐ He needs a locksmith.

e. ☐ The window is broken.

☐ She's a repair person.

4. Check (✓) the problems you sometimes have at home.

Word List: Household Problems and Repairs
Dictionary page 63

- ☐ The pipes are **frozen**
- ☐ The sink is **overflowing**
- ☐ The toilet is **stopped up**

- ☐ plumber
- ☐ exterminator
- ☐ termites

- ☐ cockroaches
- ☐ rats
- ☐ mice

5. Complete the chart. Use all the words in the Word List.

	People		Plumbing Problems		Pests
a.	plumber	c.		f.	
b.		d.		g.	
		e.		h.	
				i.	

6. Study the chart. Write the answers.

Household Problems in Vick City

roof problems 47%

plumbing problems 26%

pests: mice, cockroaches, termites 21%

Other 7%

a. What percentage of homes have plumbing problems? _____26%_____

b. What is the biggest problem in Vick City?
_____

c. Name three pests in Vick City.
_____
_____
_____

d. Name two or more plumbing problems.
_____
_____

e. Name one or more "other" problems.
_____

Challenge Which household problems can be expensive to fix?

See page 273 for listening practice.

1. **Check (✓) the words you know. Open your dictionary. Find the words you don't know.**

> ### Word List: The Tenant Meeting
> #### Dictionary pages 64-65
>
> ☐ roommates   ☐ DJ   ☐ rules   ☐ invitation
>
> ☐ party   ☐ noise   ☐ mess   ☐ **dance**
>
> ☐ music   ☐ irritated

2. **Look at the picture. Write *T* (true) or *F* (false).**

a. The people are having a party.   _F_

b. They're having a tenant meeting.   ____

c. The tenants are making some rules.   ____

d. A DJ is playing music.   ____

e. They're irritated by loud music.   ____

f. They're writing an invitation.   ____

g. The tenants are dancing.   ____

3. Look at the pictures. Circle the correct words.

a. Marvin is having a <u>meeting</u> / (party) tonight.

b. The party is for the <u>noise / tenants</u>.

c. Chad is a <u>DJ / manager</u>.

d. He's playing <u>music / rules</u>.

e. Some of the tenants are <u>dancing / irritated</u>.

f. There's <u>a big mess /a lot of noise</u>, but everybody is happy.

4. What about you? Answer the questions. Write *Yes, I do* or *No, I don't*.

a. Do you like to have parties at your home? _____.

b. Do you have rules about noise and music in your home? _____.

1. Check (✓) the things you keep in the refrigerator. Look in your dictionary for help.

Word List: Back from the Market
Dictionary pages 66–67

☐ fish   ☐ butter   ☐ bread

☐ meat   ☐ eggs   ☐ pasta

☐ chicken   ☐ vegetables   ☐ grocery bag

☐ cheese   ☐ fruit   ☐ shopping list

☐ milk   ☐ rice   ☐ coupons

2. Label the ad. Use the words in the box.

milk   ~~coupons~~   eggs   fruit   pasta   bread

Use these a. ___coupons___ and save, save, save!

b. _____

c. _____   d. _____   e. _____   f. _____

3. Read the sentences. Circle the correct words.

a. I'm back from the market. Everything is in the (grocery bags)/ coupons.

b. You can save money with coupons / a grocery bag.

c. Please put the fish / shopping list in the refrigerator.

d. Tom doesn't eat meat / milk, but he eats eggs and fish.

4. Label the pictures. Use the words in the box.

bread	cheese	eggs	fish	fruit
meat	~~milk~~	pasta	vegetables	

a. _milk_   b. _____   c. _____   d. _____   e. _____

f. _____   g. _____   h. _____   i. _____

5. Look at the picture. Complete the shopping list.

Mmm, Mmm, good for dinner tonight!

Shopping   List

a. r_ic_e_

b. chi___k___n

c. v___g___t___bles

d. b___ ___t___r

e. ch___ ___s___

Challenge Look at the shopping list. What's for dinner?

1. **Check (✓) the fruit you like to eat. Look in your dictionary for help.**

> **Word List: Fruit**
> **Dictionary page 68**
>
> ☐ apples   ☐ pears   ☐ peaches
>
> ☐ bananas   ☐ oranges   ☐ strawberries
>
> ☐ grapes   ☐ lemons   ☐ melons

2. **Unscramble the words.**

   a. cepeash   _p_ e _a_ c h _e_ _s_

   b. reasp   p __ __ r __

   c. paspel   __ p __ l e __

   d. gorenas   __ __ a __ __ e s

   e. prages   __ __ a __ e __

   f. naaansb   b __ __ a __ __ s

3. **Label the picture. Write the numbers.**

1. bananas	4. peaches	7. pears
2. strawberries	5. grapes	8. ~~apples~~
3. lemons	6. melons	9. oranges

1. Check (✓) the things you eat every week. Look in your dictionary for help.

> ### Word List: Vegetables
> #### Dictionary pages 69
>
> | | | |
> |---|---|---|
> | ☐ lettuce | ☐ peppers | ☐ potatoes |
> | ☐ carrots | ☐ celery | ☐ onions |
> | ☐ tomatoes | ☐ corn | ☐ mushrooms |

2. Look at the picture. Circle the vegetables. Then write the answers.

a. How many peppers are there?   3

b. How many tomatoes are there?   ___

c. How many onions are there?   ___

d. How many potatoes are there?   ___

e. How many types of vegetables are there?   ___

3. Look at the pictures. Write the recipes.

a. Four Veggie Juice

1 _____

5 _____

4 _____

3 _____

b. Hot Days Juice

1 cup _____lettuce_____

1 _____

1 red _____

c. Sweet Dreams Juice

3 _____

4 _____

2 stalks _____

1 cup _____

Challenge Circle the juice you want to try.

Meat and Poultry

1. Check (✓) the things in your refrigerator now. Look in your dictionary for help.

Word List: Meat and Poultry
Dictionary page 70

Beef
- ☐ roast
- ☐ steak
- ☐ ground beef

Pork
- ☐ ham
- ☐ bacon
- ☐ sausage

Lamb
- ☐ lamb chops

Poultry
- ☐ chicken
- ☐ turkey

2. Complete the menu. Use the words in the box.

meat   ~~steak~~   ham   bacon   sausage   lamb chops   chicken   turkey

Benny's Restaurant

BREAKFAST – *Your choice* **$6.99**

a. _____ and eggs

b. _____ and eggs

c. _____ and eggs

LUNCH – *Your choice* **$8.99**

Hamburger

d. __steak__ sandwich

e. _____ and salad

DINNER – *Your choice* **$10.99**

f. _____ dinner

g. _____

We make vegetarian dinners.

h. No _____ !

3. Use the menu in Exercise 2. Answer the questions. Write *yes* or *no*.

a. Is there pork on the menu? ___yes___

b. Is there ground beef on the menu? _____

c. Is there roast on the menu? _____

d. Is there poultry on the menu? _____

e. Is there fruit on the menu? _____

70

1. Check (✓) the things you like to eat. Look in your dictionary for help.

Word List: Seafood and Deli
Dictionary page 71

☐ salmon	☐ wheat bread	☐ processed cheese
☐ shrimp	☐ roast beef	☐ Swiss cheese
☐ frozen fish	☐ smoked turkey	☐ cheddar cheese

2. Complete the chart. Use the words in the box.

roast beef   shrimp   processed cheese   ~~frozen fish~~   cheddar cheese   smoked turkey

Seafood	Meat	Cheese
a. frozen fish	c.	e.
b.	d.	f.

3. Look at the pictures. Circle the correct words.

a. Rebecca likes
smoked turkey /
(roast beef.)

b. Armando likes
Swiss cheese /
roast beef.

c. Sam likes smoked turkey/
fish.

d. Wilma likes
cheddar cheese /
wheat bread.

e. Su Ling likes
salmon / shrimp.

f. Charlie likes frozen fish /
cheddar cheese.

1. **Check (✓) the words you know. Look in your dictionary. Find the words you don't know.**

> ## Word List: A Grocery Store
> ### Dictionary pages 72–73
>
> | | | |
> |---|---|---|
> | ☐ customer | **Canned Foods** | **Baking Products** |
> | ☐ aisle | ☐ beans | ☐ flour |
> | ☐ cart | ☐ tuna | ☐ sugar |
> | ☐ manager | **Dairy** | ☐ oil |
> | ☐ line | ☐ yogourt | **Baked Goods** |
> | ☐ cashier | **Frozen Foods** | ☐ cookies |
> | ☐ bagger | ☐ ice cream | ☐ cake |

2. **Cross out the word that doesn't belong.**

   a. customer ~~ice cream~~ bagger   **d.** ice cream cake tuna

   b. manager line aisle   **e.** beans flour sugar

   c. tuna beans cashier   **f.** yogourt flour ice cream

3. **Label the pictures. Use the words in the box.**

yogourt	bagger	cookies	~~customer~~	manager	tuna

   a. ___customer___   b. _____   c. _____

   d. _____   e. _____   f. _____

4. Look at the picture. Write *T* (true) or *F* (false).

a. There are three customers.   _T_

b. The cashier is happy.   ___

c. Two customers have carts.   ___

d. The man is buying a bottle of oil.   ___

e. He's also buying cookies.   ___

f. Two women are in line.   ___

g. The bagger is happy.   ___

5. Look at the store directory. Answer the questions.

a. Where can you find canned beans?   _aisle 2_

b. Where can you find cookies?   _____

c. Where can you find yogourt?   _____

d. Where can you find sugar?   _____

e. Where can you find turkey and cheese?   _____

f. Where can you find ice cream?   _____

g. Where can you find milk?   _____

h. Where can you find vegetables?   _____

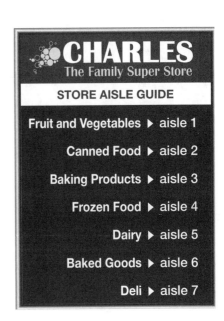

CHARLES
The Family Super Store

STORE AISLE GUIDE

Fruit and Vegetables ▶ aisle 1

Canned Food ▶ aisle 2

Baking Products ▶ aisle 3

Frozen Food ▶ aisle 4

Dairy ▶ aisle 5

Baked Goods ▶ aisle 6

Deli ▶ aisle 7

Challenge Name two places in the grocery store where the food is cold.

1. Check (✓) the things you have in the refrigerator. Look in your dictionary for help.

> ### Word List: Containers and Packaged Foods
> #### Dictionary page 74
>
> ☐ bottle　　　☐ container　　　☐ a carton of eggs
> ☐ jar　　　　☐ box　　　　　☐ a six-pack of pop
> ☐ can　　　　☐ bag　　　　　☐ a loaf of bread

2. Complete the words. Write the letters.

a. j a _r_

b. ___ ___ x

c. ___ ___ g

d. ___ ___ n

e. b ___ ___ t l ___

f. c ___ n ___ a ___ n ___ ___

g. c ___ r ___ ___ n

h. l ___ ___ f

3. Label the picture. Write the numbers.

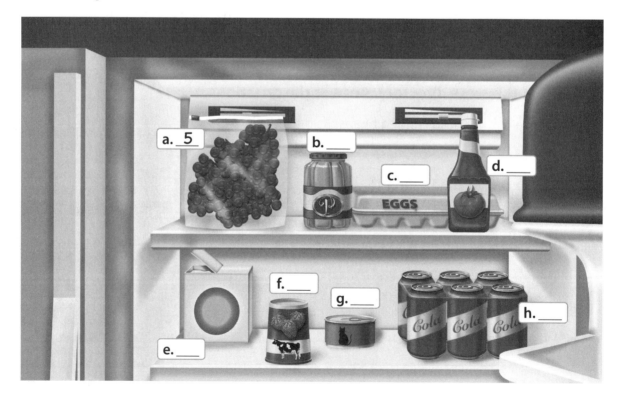

a. _5_　　b. ___　　c. ___　　d. ___　　e. ___　　f. ___　　g. ___　　h. ___

EGGS

Cola Cola Cola

1. bottle　　**3.** container　　**5.** ~~bag~~　　**7.** jar

2. can　　　**4.** box　　　　**6.** carton　　**8.** six-pack

 See page 276 for listening practice.

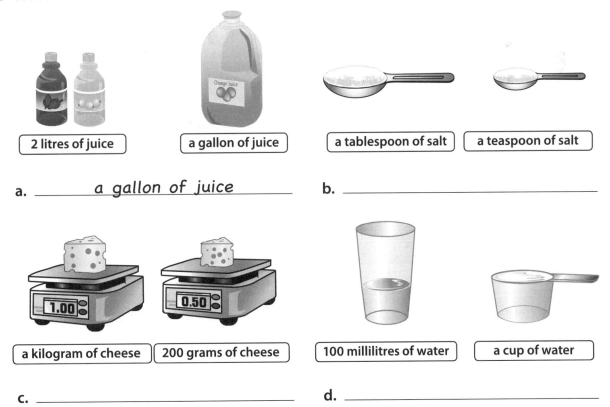

1. **Check (✓) the words you know. Look in your dictionary. Find the words you don't know.**

> ## Word List: Weights and Measures
> ### Dictionary page 75
>
> ☐ a cup of oil   ☐ a 4-litre jug of water   ☐ a cup of flour
>
> ☐ 500 millilitres   ☐ a teaspoon of salt   ☐ 500 grams of cheese
> of frozen yogourt
>   ☐ a tablespoon of sugar   ☐ a kilogram of
> ☐ a litre of milk   roast beef

2. **Match the words with the abbreviations.**

| L | mL | ~~c.~~ | kg | tsp. | oz. | gal. | tbsp. |

a. cup __c.__   c. millilitre _____   e. teaspoon _____   g. ounce _____

b. litre _____   d. gallon _____   f. tablespoon _____   h. kilogram _____

3. **Which is more? Write the answers.**

| 2 litres of juice | a gallon of juice | a tablespoon of salt | a teaspoon of salt |

a. ___a gallon of juice___   b. _____

| a kilogram of cheese | 200 grams of cheese | 100 millilitres of water | a cup of water |

c. _____   d. _____

Challenge How many litres are in a gallon? How many grams are in a kilogram?

75

Food Preparation and Safety

1. Check (✓) the words you know. Look in your dictionary. Find the words you don't know.

Word List: Food Preparation and Safety
Dictionary page 76

☐ clean	☐ fried	☐ boiled
☐ cook	☐ barbecued	☐ stir-fried
☐ chill	☐ roasted	☐ scrambled

2. Unscramble the words.

a. bolied *b* o *i* l e *d*

b. steorad r ___ a s ___ ___ d

c. diref ___ r i ___ ___

d. ilhlc ___ ___ ___ ___ l

e. ancle ___ ___ e a ___

f. okoc c ___ ___ ___

3. Label the picture. Use the words in the box.

fried	barbecued	scrambled	stir-fried	~~roasted~~	boiled

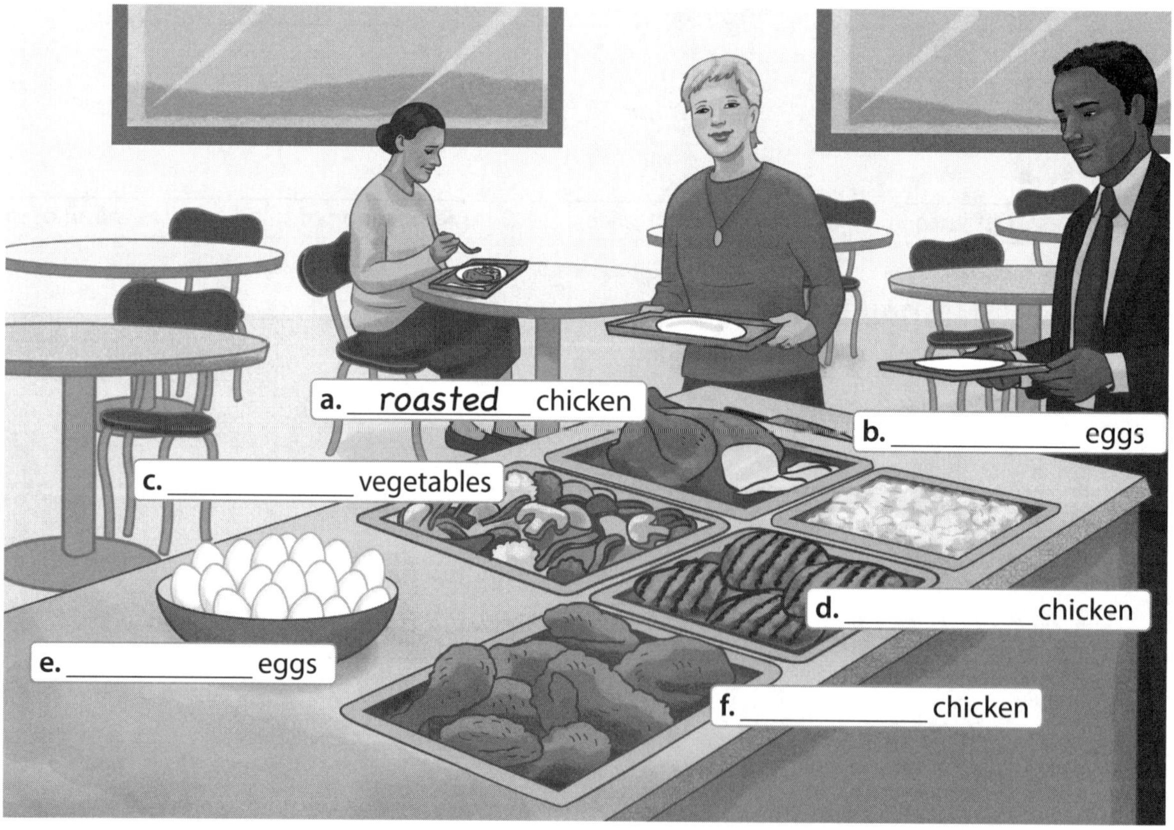

a. *roasted* chicken
b. ______ eggs
c. ______ vegetables
d. ______ chicken
e. ______ eggs
f. ______ chicken

4. Check (✓) the things you do to prepare your favourite food. Look in your dictionary for help.

> **Word List: Food Preparation and Safety**
> Dictionary page 77
>
> ☐ preheat   ☐ bake   ☐ chop
> ☐ slice   ☐ cut up   ☐ boil
> ☐ steam   ☐ peel   ☐ mix

5. How do you prepare these foods? Check (✓) the correct words.

a. ☐ mix   ☑ peel
b. ☐ boil   ☐ slice
c. ☐ chop   ☐ bake
d. ☐ steam ☐ preheat

6. Look at the pictures. Complete the recipe. Use the words in the box.

| Mix | Slice | Peel | ~~Preheat~~ | Cut up | Chop |

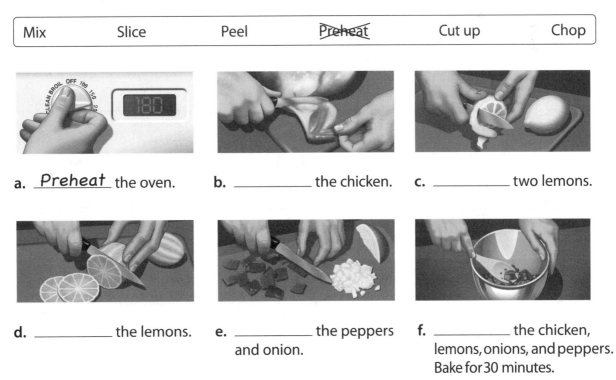

a. __Preheat__ the oven.

b. _____ the chicken.

c. _____ two lemons.

d. _____ the lemons.

e. _____ the peppers and onion.

f. _____ the chicken, lemons, onions, and peppers. Bake for 30 minutes.

See page 277 for listening practice.

1. Check (✓) the things you have in your kitchen. Look in your dictionary for help.

Word List: Kitchen Utensils
Dictionary page 78

☐ can opener   ☐ frying pan   ☐ vegetable peeler

☐ grater   ☐ pot   ☐ lid

☐ steamer   ☐ wooden spoon   ☐ mixing bowl

2. Match the words with the pictures.

1.

2.

3.

4.

5.

6.

_4_ **a.** steamer   ___ **c.** frying pan   ___ **e.** pot

___ **b.** can opener   ___ **d.** lid   ___ **f.** wooden spoon

3. Complete the sentences. Use the words in the box.

| mixing bowl   can opener   ~~frying pan~~   peeler   lid   grater |

a. I need a _frying pan_.   **b.** I need a _____.   **c.** I need a _____.

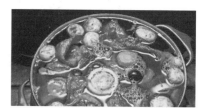

d. I need a _____.   **e.** I need a _____.   **f.** I need a _____.

1. Check (✓) your three favourite fast foods. Look in your dictionary for help.

Word List: Fast Food Restaurant
Dictionary page 79

☐ hamburger   ☐ hot dog   ☐ pizza

☐ french fries   ☐ nachos   ☐ pop

☐ cheeseburger   ☐ taco   ☐ doughnut

2. Complete the menu. Use the words in the box.

| hot dog | ~~nachos~~ | taco | soda | pizza | doughnuts |

Fast Freddy's Snacks and Things

a. _nachos_ — $1.99

b. _____ — $1.99

c. _____ — $1.49

d. _____ — 99¢ each

e. _____ — $2.29

f. _____ — 99¢

3. Study the graph. Answer the questions.

a. What is the favourite fast food for girls? _french fries_

b. What is the favourite fast food for boys? _____

c. Which food is equally popular for boys and girls? _____

d. Look at the Word List. Name an example of "other" fast food. _____

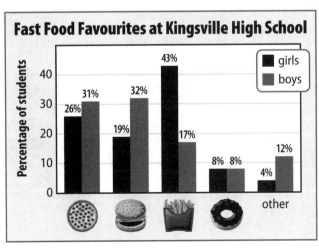

Fast Food Favourites at Kingsville High School

girls ■ boys ■

26% 31% / 19% 32% / 43% 17% / 8% 8% / 4% 12%

Percentage of students

other

Challenge Look at the menu in Exercise 2. Write your order and the total price.

1. Check (✓) the things you like to eat and drink. Look in your dictionary for help.

> **Word List: Coffee Shop Menu**
> **Dictionary pages 80-81**
>
> ☐ breakfast ☐ toast ☐ sandwich ☐ spaghetti
> ☐ lunch ☐ pancakes ☐ salad ☐ meatballs
> ☐ dinner ☐ cereal ☐ soup ☐ grilled fish
> ☐ dessert ☐ cake ☐ coffee ☐ meatloaf
> ☐ beverages ☐ pie ☐ tea

2. Match the words.

_2_ **a.** dinner   **1.** soup and a sandwich

___ **b.** lunch   **2.** spaghetti and meatballs

___ **c.** beverage   **3.** cake

___ **d.** breakfast   **4.** pancakes

___ **e.** dessert   **5.** tea

3. Label the picture with the numbers.

a. _4_

b. ___

c. ___

d. ___

e. ___

f. ___

1. They're having soup and salad.

2. They're having meatloaf and vegetables.

3. She's having cereal and tea.

4. She's having coffee and toast.

5. They're having sandwiches.

6. She's having pancakes and eggs.

4. Look at the picture. Complete the bill. Then answer the questions.

Guest Bill

DATE	TABLE	GUESTS	SERVER	223458

APPT-SOUP/SAL-ENTREE-VEG/POT-DESSERT-BEV

	g r i l l e d f i s h	$9.99
	s _ a g _ e t _ _ _ a n d	
	m _ a t _ a _ _ _ s	$7.99
	c _ k _	$3.99
	p _ _	$3.99
2	c _ f f _ _ _ s	$1.98
	TAX	
	TOTAL	

THANK YOU - PLEASE COME AGAIN.

a. How much is dessert?   <u>$7.98</u>

b. How much are the beverages?   _____

c. Which item is $9.99?   _____

d. Is this breakfast, lunch, or dinner?   _____

5. What about you? Answer the questions.

a. What is the name of your favourite restaurant?   _____

b. Is that restaurant a coffee shop?   _____

c. What do you usually order there?   _____

d. Do you usually go there for breakfast, lunch, or dinner?   _____

See page 278 for listening practice.

1. **Check (✓) the words you know. Look in your dictionary. Find the words you don't know.**

> ### Word List: A Restaurant
> #### Dictionary pages 82–83
>
> | | | |
> |---|---|---|
> | ☐ hostess | ☐ **set** the table | ☐ **pay** the bill |
> | ☐ high chair | ☐ **seat** the customer | ☐ **leave** a tip |
> | ☐ booth | ☐ **order** from the menu | |
> | ☐ menu | ☐ **take** the order | |
> | ☐ server | ☐ **serve** the meal | |
> | ☐ busser | ☐ **clear** the dishes | |

2. **Complete the chart. Use the words in the box.**

> ~~menu~~   serve   table   pay   order   clear   dishes

Customer	Server	Busser
a. order from the __menu__	c. take the _____	e. set the _____
b. _____ the bill	d. _____ the meal	f. _____ the _____

3. **Look at the picture. Write _T_ (true) or _F_ (false).**

a. The menus are on the table. __T__

b. The server is at the table. ____

c. There's a high chair at the table. ____

d. They want to pay the bill. ____

e. They want to order now. ____

f. They're leaving a tip. ____

4. Read the sentences. Label the picture with the numbers.

1. Carmen is a customer. She needs a high chair for the baby.

2. Lee is a server. He's taking an order.

3. Joe is a busser. He's setting a table.

4. Al is sitting in a booth with his friend.

5. Nora is a hostess. She's seating a customer.

6. Iris is a busser. She's clearing a table.

7. Pablo is paying the bill.

8. Ina is a server. She's serving a meal.

5. Read the ads. Circle the correct words.

HELP WANTED
at family restaurant.
Take orders, serve food. Must learn menu. Free lunch, good tips.
555-3254 days.

RESTAURANT HELP
WANTED
Set tables and clear dishes, clean booths. Some tips, good hours. **314 Main St.**

a. This job is for a <u>hostess</u> / (<u>server</u>)

b. At this restaurant the customers leave good <u>lunch</u> / <u>tips</u>.

c. You need to study the <u>menu</u> / <u>server</u> for this job.

d. This job is for a <u>busser</u> / <u>hostess</u>.

e. You need to clear <u>high chair</u> / <u>dishes</u> and clean <u>orders</u> / <u>booths</u> at this job.

f. You get some <u>lunch</u> / <u>tips</u> at this job.

1. **Check (✓) the words you know. Look in your dictionary. Find the words you don't know.**

> ### Word List: The Farmers' Market
> #### Dictionary pages 84–85
>
> ☐ live music ☐ sour ☐ vendors ☐ herbs
>
> ☐ organic ☐ samples ☐ sweets ☐ **count**
>
> ☐ lemonade ☐ avocados

2. **Match the words with the pictures.**

_1_ **a.** sweets   ___ **e.** vendor

___ **b.** organic herbs   ___ **f.** avocados

___ **c.** sour lemonade   ___ **g.** count

___ **d.** live music   ___ **h.** samples

3. Look at the pictures. Circle the correct words.

a. We go to the ⟨farmers'⟩ / sweet market every Sunday.

b. I like the <u>live / sour</u> music.

c. My son likes the free <u>samples / vendors</u>.

d. We buy <u>organic / sour</u> vegetables there.

e. Sometimes we <u>buy herbs / count vendors</u>.

f. Today we are buying <u>samples / avocados</u>.

g. My son is drinking <u>lemonade / avocados</u>. It's sweet.

h. I'm <u>counting / buying</u> my money.

4. What about you? Answer the questions. Write *Yes, there is* or *No, there isn't*.

a. Is there a farmers' market near your home? _____

b. Is there a place to buy organic food near your home? _____

c. Is there a place to listen to live music near your home? _____

Everyday Clothes

1. **Check (✓) the words you know. Look in your dictionary. Find the words you don't know.**

2. **Cross out the word that doesn't belong.**

a.	shirt	~~socks~~	blouse
b.	sweater	shoes	athletic shoes
c.	pants	jeans	shirt
d.	skirt	baseball cap	dress
e.	suit	T-shirt	dress
f.	tie shoes	put on socks	handbag

3. **Look at the ad. Complete the sentences. Use the words in the box.**

T-shirts   sweaters   blouses   handbags   pants   ~~shirts~~

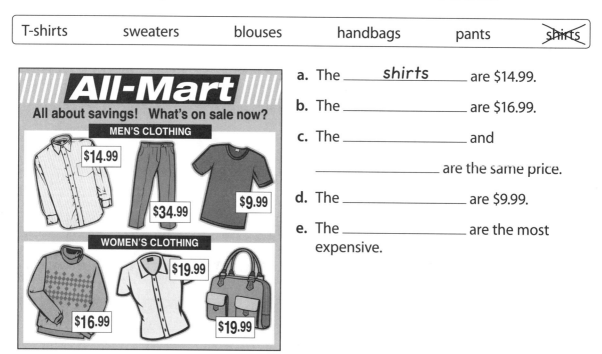

a. The _____shirts_____ are $14.99.

b. The _____ are $16.99.

c. The _____ and

_____ are the same price.

d. The _____ are $9.99.

e. The _____ are the most
expensive.

4. Look at the pictures. Check (✓) the correct sentences.

a. ☐ He's wearing a T-shirt.

☑ He's wearing jeans.

b. ☐ She has a handbag.

☐ She's wearing pants and a shirt.

c. ☐ Three students are wearing jeans.

☐ Three students are wearing T-shirts.

d. ☐ He's putting on his socks.

☐ He can tie his shoes.

e. ☐ They're wearing socks and jeans.

☐ They're wearing athletic shoes and caps.

f. ☐ She's wearing a skirt and blouse.

☐ He's wearing a suit.

5. Study the chart. Answer the questions.

a. What percentage of people like jeans the best? __56%__

b. What percentage like dresses or suits the best? _____

c. What percentage like pants and shirts the best? _____

d. What percentage of people don't like jeans the best? _____

Favourite Clothes at Baker Adult School

56%

23%

16%

5%

other

Casual, Work, and Formal Clothes

1. **Check (✓) the things you like to wear. Look in your dictionary for help.**

> **Word List: Casual, Work, and Formal Clothes**
> **Dictionary pages 88–89**
>
> ☐ overalls ☐ uniform ☐ tuxedo ☐ sweatshirt
> ☐ knit top ☐ business suit ☐ evening gown ☐ sweatpants
> ☐ sandals ☐ briefcase ☐ tank top
> ☐ tie ☐ shorts

2. **Unscramble the words.**

   a. storsh   s h _o_ _r_ t s

   b. slandsa   s ___ n d ___ ___ s

   c. iformnu   u ___ i f ___ ___ ___

   d. vorllaes   ___ v e ___ a ___ ___ s

   e. otuxed   t ___ x ___ ___ ___

   f. tehsrwiats   s w___ ___ ___ s ___ ___ ___ t

   g. ktan opt   ___ ___ ___ ___   ___ ___ ___

   h. enevgin wnog   ___ ___ ___ ___ ___ ___   ___ ___ ___ ___

3. **Label the picture. Write the numbers.**

   1. briefcase
   2. business suit
   3. knit top
   4. overalls

a. 2
b. ___
c. ___
d. ___

Challenge Look at the picture above. Name the shoes you see.

88

4. Look at the picture. Read the sentences. Number the people.

a. _2_

b. ____

c. ____

d. ____

e. ____

f. ____

g. ____

1. Jack is wearing a uniform.

2. Gabriel is wearing a business suit.

3. Ken is wearing shorts.

4. Lara is wearing overalls.

5. Grace is wearing sweatpants.

6. Anne is wearing sandals.

7. Jen is looking at a dress.

5. What about you? Complete the sentences with *casual, work,* or *formal*.

a. I like _____ clothes.

b. I think _____ clothes are expensive.

c. I think _____ clothes are comfortable.

d. I don't like to wear _____ clothes.

e. I usually wear _____ clothes.

See page 279 for listening practice.

1. **Check (✓) the things you never wear or use. Look in your dictionary for help.**

Word List: Seasonal Clothing
Dictionary page 90

☐ coat	☐ jacket	☐ raincoat
☐ scarf	☐ hat	☐ swimsuit
☐ gloves	☐ umbrella	☐ sunglasses

2. **Complete the chart. Use the words in the box.**

gloves	raincoat	~~coat~~	sunglasses
umbrella	scarf	swimsuit	

Cold	Rainy	Hot
a. *coat*	d.	f.
b.	e.	g.
c.		

3. **Look at the picture. Circle the correct words.**

   a. The girl is wearing a (scarf) / hat.

   b. The boy is wearing a hat / sunglasses.

   c. The boy and the girl are wearing coats / swimsuits.

   d. The boy and the girl are wearing raincoats / gloves.

   e. Sam has an umbrella / sunglasses.

   f. Sam is wearing a jacket / scarf.

Underwear and Sleepwear

1. Check (✓) the words you know. Look in your dictionary. Find the words you don't know.

Word List: Underwear and Sleepwear
Dictionary page 91

☐ undershirt ☐ socks ☐ bra ☐ nightgown
☐ boxer shorts ☐ panties ☐ pyjamas ☐ robe
☐ briefs ☐ pantyhose

2. Match the words with the pictures.

1.  2.  3.

4.  5.   6.

_4_ **a.** boxer shorts ___ **c.** socks ___ **e.** undershirt

___ **b.** bra ___ **d.** panty hose ___ **f.** briefs

3. Label the picture. Use the words in the box.

| boxer shorts | ~~socks~~ | pantyhose | pyjamas | nightgown | robe |

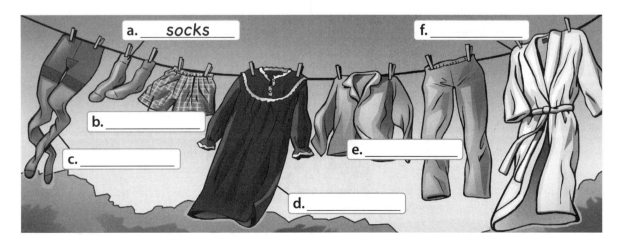

a. ___socks___   f. _____
b. _____
c. _____   e. _____
d. _____

91

Workplace Clothing

1. **Check (✓) the things you or your classmates wear at work.
   Look in your dictionary for help.**

   > ### Word List: Workplace Clothing
   > #### Dictionary pages 92–93
   >
   > | | | |
   > |---|---|---|
   > | ☐ hard hat | ☐ apron | ☐ hairnet |
   > | ☐ work shirt | ☐ polo shirt | ☐ scrubs |
   > | ☐ tool belt | ☐ name tag | ☐ face mask |
   > | ☐ coveralls | ☐ work gloves | ☐ lab coat |
   > | ☐ safety glasses | ☐ badge | ☐ latex gloves |

2. **Match the words.**

   _5_ **a.** hard   **1.** mask

   ___ **b.** face   **2.** coat

   ___ **c.** lab   **3.** belt

   ___ **d.** tool   **4.** tag

   ___ **e.** polo   **5.** hat

   ___ **f.** name   **6.** shirt

3. **Label the pictures. Use the words in the box.**

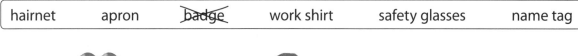

   | hairnet | apron | ~~badge~~ | work shirt | safety glasses | name tag |

   a. _____badge_____   b. _____   c. _____

   d. _____   e. _____   f. _____

4. **Look at the picture. Write *T* (true) or *F* (false).**

a. There's a glove on the floor. _T_

b. There's a man in coveralls. ____

c. There's a worker with safety glasses. ____

d. There's a woman in scrubs. ____

e. There's a doctor in an apron. ____

f. There are two people with gloves. ____

5. **Look at the picture. Write three things John needs to be safe.**

a. _____

b. _____

c. _____

Shoes and Accessories

1. **Check (✓) the words you know. Look in your dictionary. Find the words you don't know.**

Word List: Shoes and Accessories
Dictionary pages 94–95

☐ purses   ☐ necklaces   ☐ pumps

☐ belts   ☐ wallet   ☐ boots

☐ shoe department   ☐ watch   ☐ tennis shoes

☐ jewellery department   ☐ backpack   ☐ earrings

☐ bracelets   ☐ high heels   ☐ ring

2. **Complete the chart. Use the words in the box.**

backpacks	wallets	boots	earrings	tennis shoes
high heels	necklaces	purses	~~rings~~	

Jewellery Department	Shoe Department	Other Accessories
a. *rings*	d.	g.
b.	e.	h.
c.	f.	i.

3. **Read the sentences. Write *T* (true) or *F* (false).**

   a. You can buy earrings in the shoe department.   _F_

   b. Many children use backpacks at school.   ____

   c. Bracelets and pumps are in the jewellery department. ____

   d. Boots and high heels are in the shoe department.   ____

   e. People keep money in their watches.   ____

   f. People wear tennis shoes to exercise.   ____

4. Look at the picture. Circle the correct words.

a. The girl has a (purse)/ backpack.

b. The girl is wearing a watch / belt.

c. The woman is wearing boots / pumps.

d. The girl is wearing tennis shoes / high heels.

e. There are tennis shoes / boots on the floor.

5. Look at the receipt. Complete the sentences.

```
               NICKELS
          DEPARTMENT STORE
-----------------------------------
01  MEN'S  TENNIS SHOES      $24.99
02  CHILDREN'S SHOES 2@ $10.99  $21.98
03  BOOTS                    $36.98
04  WOMEN'S ACCESSORIES: PURSE  $24.50
05  FASHION JEWELLERY: RING    $12.99
06  FASHION JEWELLERY: NECKLACE  $ 9.99
                  SUBTOTAL  $131.43
                       TAX   $11.50
                     TOTAL  $142.93
```

a. The ___boots___ cost $36.98.

b. The _____ is from the accessories department.

c. The total for jewellery is _____.

d. The total from the shoe department is _____.

Challenge Name the shoes and accessories you wear and use every day.

See page 280 for listening practice.

Describing Clothes

1. **Check (✓) the words that describe the clothes you wear. Look in your dictionary for help**

Word List: Describing Clothes
Dictionary page 96

☐ small   ☐ short-sleeved   ☐ solid
☐ medium   ☐ long-sleeved   ☐ striped
☐ large   ☐ short
               ☐ long

2. **Match the words with the pictures.**

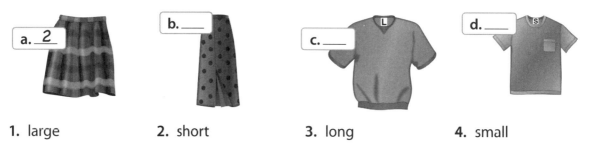

a. _2_   b. ____   c. ____   d. ____

1. large   2. short   3. long   4. small

3. **Read the story. Put the pictures in order (1–6).**

Bita needs a new shirt. She looks at a long-sleeved white shirt. She looks at a short-sleeved white shirt. She looks at another shirt. It's striped. Then Bita sees a solid black shirt. She likes it the best! She buys a medium.

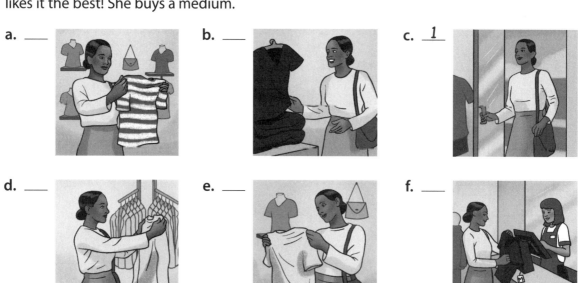

a. ____   b. ____   c. _1_

d. ____   e. ____   f. ____

4. **Check (✓) the words you know. Look in your dictionary. Find the words you don't know.**

Word List: Describing Clothes
Dictionary page 97

☐ heavy   ☐ loose   ☐ too small

☐ light   ☐ narrow   ☐ too big

☐ tight   ☐ wide   ☐ too expensive

5. **Match the opposites.**

a. heavy   __3__   1. too big

b. tight   ____   2. narrow

c. wide   ____   3. light

d. too small   ____   4. loose

6. **Look at the pictures. Complete the sentences. Use the words in the box.**

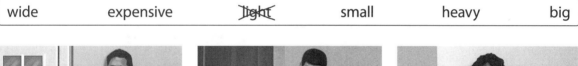

wide   expensive   ~~light~~   small   heavy   big

a. His jacket is ___*light*___.

b. The shirt is too _____.

c. Her sweater is _____.

d. The dress is too _____.

e. His tie is _____.

f. His pants are too _____.

Making Clothes

1. **Check (✓) the words you know. Look in your dictionary. Find the words you don't know.**

> ## Word List: Making Clothes
> ### Dictionary pages 98–99
>
> ☐ cotton   ☐ **sew**   ☐ pattern
> ☐ wool   ☐ sewing machine   ☐ thread
> ☐ leather   ☐ sewing machine operator   ☐ button
> ☐ denim   ☐ needle   ☐ zipper
>   ☐ snap

2. **Label the pictures. Use the words in the box.**

| ~~cotton~~ | wool | leather | denim |

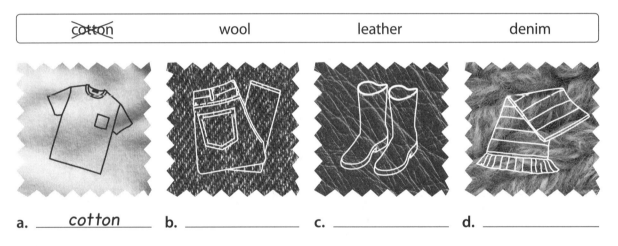

a. ___cotton___   b. _____   c. _____   d. _____

3. **Look at the picture. Write *T* (true) or *F* (false).**

a. The man is using a pattern.   __T__

b. The women are sewing machine operators.   ____

c. The women are sewing skirts.   ____

d. The man is working with leather.   ____

e. The women are not sewing right now.   ____

Challenge Look at Exercise 2. Name two types of material you like to wear.

4. Label the picture. Write the numbers.

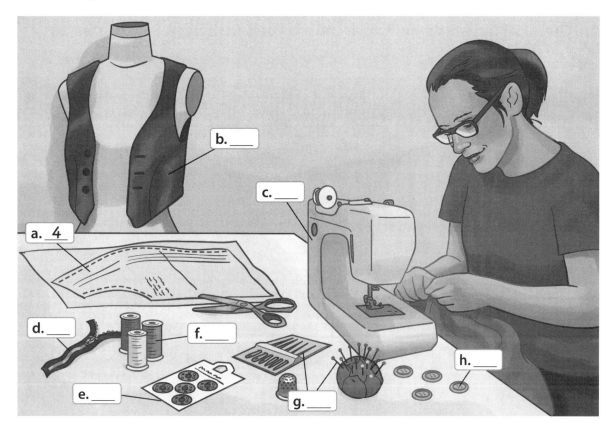

a. _4_   b. ____   c. ____   d. ____   e. ____   f. ____   g. ____   h. ____

1. button	3. needle	5. sewing machine	7. thread
2. leather	4. ~~pattern~~	6. snap	8. zipper

5. Read the sentences. Check (✓) the things the people need.

a. Beatriz wants to make a dress for summer. What does she need?

✓ cotton material   ☐ wool

✓ a pattern   ✓ a sewing machine

b. Sam wants to sew a button on his shirt. What does he need?

☐ a buckle   ☐ a button

☐ thread   ☐ a needle

c. Amy needs a new zipper in her dress. What does she need?

☐ a sewing machine   ☐ material

☐ a zipper   ☐ snaps

d. Lia wants to make jeans. What does she need?

☐ denim   ☐ a zipper

☐ a pattern   ☐ a button

Making Alterations

1. **Check (✓) the words you know. Look in your dictionary. Find the words you don't know.**

Word List: Making Alterations
Dictionary page 100

- ☐ pocket
- ☐ hem
- ☐ pin
- ☐ safety pin
- ☐ scissors
- ☐ **lengthen**
- ☐ **shorten**
- ☐ **let out**
- ☐ take in

2. **Match the words with the pictures.**

1.   2.   3.   4.   5.

_4_ **a.** hem   ___ **b.** pocket   ___ **c.** pin   ___ **d.** safety pin   ___ **e.** scissors

3. **Look at the pictures. Complete the sentences. Use the words in the box.**

| lengthen | take in | let out | pocket | shorten | ~~scissors~~ |

a. She needs a pair of _scissors_.

b. She needs to _____ the dress.

c. He needs to sew the _____.

d. She needs to _____ the pants.

e. He needs to _____ the pants.

f. She needs to _____ the dress.

Doing the Laundry

1. Check (✓) the things you use and the things you do. Look in your dictionary for help.

Word List: Doing the Laundry
Dictionary page 101

☐ laundry ☐ hanger ☐ **Fold** the laundry
☐ washer ☐ iron ☐ **Iron** the clothes
☐ dryer ☐ ironing board ☐ **Hang up** the clothes

2. Complete the sentences. Use the words in the box.

laundry ~~washer~~ dryer ironing board hangers fold

a. It's time to wash the clothes. Put the laundry in the _washer_.

b. I need to iron my shirt. Where is the _____?

c. David and Parvin do the _____ every Saturday.

d. We need to dry the clothes. Please put the clothes in the _____.

e. Sam needs some _____. He wants to hang up his shirts.

f. The clothes in the dryer are dry. It's time to _____ the laundry.

3. Look at the story. Put the sentences in order (1-6).

____ He puts the clothes in the washer.

_1_ Ali needs to do the laundry.

____ He folds some of the clothes.

____ He hangs up the shirts.

____ He puts the clothes in the dryer.

____ He irons the shirts.

See page 281 for listening practice. 101

A Garage Sale

1. **Check (✓) the words you know. Look in your dictionary. Find the words you don't know.**

<table>
<tr><td colspan="3">Word List: A Garage Sale
Dictionary pages 102–103</td></tr>
<tr><td>☐ flyer</td><td>☐ folding card table</td><td>☐ VCR</td></tr>
<tr><td>☐ used clothing</td><td>☐ folding chair</td><td>☐ bargain</td></tr>
<tr><td>☐ sticker</td><td>☐ clock radio</td><td>☐ browse</td></tr>
</table>

2. **Match the words with the pictures.**

_6_ **a.** flyer

1.

___ **b.** folding chair

2.

___ **c.** stickers

3.

___ **d.** VCR

4.

___ **e.** clock radio

5.

___ **f.** bargain

6.

___ **g.** card table

7.

3. Look at the pictures. Circle the correct words.

a. The Chiu family has a clock radio / (garage sale) every year.

b. They make a <u>flyer</u> / sticker together.

c. They put price <u>sales</u> / <u>stickers</u> on all their old things.

d. They put a <u>card table</u> / flyer and two <u>folding chairs</u> / VCRs in the yard.

e. This year they have a lot of <u>used clothing</u> / stickers for sale.

f. Mr. Chiu wants to sell an old <u>VCR</u> / clock radio.

g. Many people come to <u>browse</u> / help.

h. The customers like to <u>browse</u> / <u>bargain</u> with Mrs. Chiu.

4. What about you? Answer the questions. Write _Yes, I do_ or _No, I don't_.

a. Do you like to go to garage sales? _____

b. Do you like to have garage sales? _____

c. Do you like to bargain when you shop? _____

1. **Check (✓) the parts of the body that are below the neck. Use your dictionary for help.**

Word List: The Body
Dictionary pages 104-105

☐ head   ☐ back   ☐ leg   ☐ shoulder

☐ hair   ☐ nose   ☐ toe   ☐ arm

☐ neck   ☐ mouth   ☐ eye   ☐ hand

☐ chest   ☐ foot   ☐ ear   ☐ finger

2. **Cross out the word that doesn't belong.**

   a. eye   nose   ~~foot~~   mouth

   b. leg   neck   toe   foot

   c. back   arm   hand   finger

   d. chest   back   eye   shoulder

   e. head   hair   ear   leg

3. **Label the picture. Write the numbers.**

   1. arm
   2. back
   3. chest
   4. head
   5. eye
   6. leg
   7. ear
   8. hand
   9. ~~hair~~
   10. mouth

a. 9
b. ___
c. ___
d. ___
e. ___
f. ___
g. ___
h. ___
i. ___
j. ___

4. Look at the picture. Read the sentences. Write the numbers.

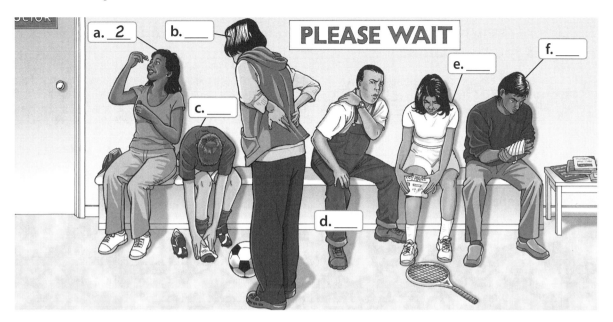

1. Jack has a problem with his foot.
2. Mary has a problem with her eye.
3. Rosa has a problem with her knee.

4. Sun has a problem with her back.
5. Jin has a problem with his shoulder.
6. Tej has a problem with his hand.

5. Study the graph. Answer the questions.

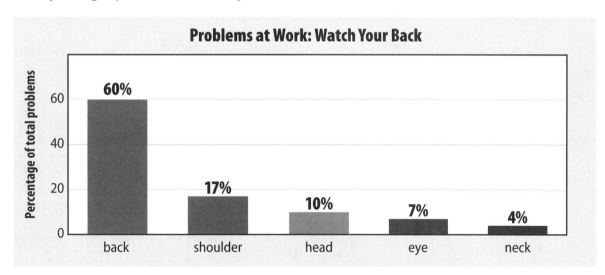

a. Sixty percent of the problems at work are _____*back*_____ problems.

b. Ten percent of the problems are with the _____.

c. _____ percent of the problems are eye problems.

d. Twenty-one percent of problems are with the shoulder and the _____.

e. Eleven percent of problems are _____ and _____ problems.

Inside and Outside the Body

1. **Check (✓) the words you know. Open your dictionary. Find the words you don't know.**

The Face	The Arm	The Senses
☐ chin	☐ elbow	☐ see
☐ forehead	☐ wrist	☐ hear
The Mouth	**The Leg**	☐ smell
☐ lip	☐ knee	☐ taste
☐ teeth	☐ ankle	☐ touch
☐ tongue		

2. **Match the words with the pictures.**

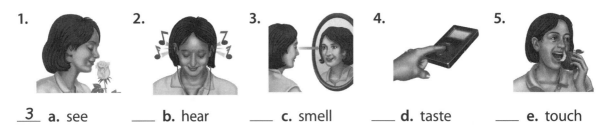

_3_ a. see   ___ b. hear   ___ c. smell   ___ d. taste   ___ e. touch

3. **Label the picture. Write the numbers.**

1. forehead
2. ~~chin~~
3. lip
4. teeth
5. tongue
6. elbow
7. wrist
8. knee
9. ankle

Challenge Which senses help you learn English?

4. **Check (✓) the things that are inside the chest. Use your dictionary for help.**

Word List: Inside and Outside the Body
Dictionary page 107

☐ muscle   ☐ heart   ☐ stomach

☐ bone   ☐ lung   ☐ kidney

☐ brain   ☐ liver

5. **Complete the words. Write the letters.**

a. h _e_ a r _t_

b. b r __ __ n

c. k i __ __ e y

d. l __ __ __ r

e. m __ s __ __ e

f. s t o __ __ c __

6. **Look at the picture. Write _T_ (true) or _F_ (false). Use your dictionary for help.**

a. The liver is above the lungs.   _F_

b. The heart is between the lungs.   ____

c. The lungs are in the stomach.   ____

d. The brain is in the head.   ____

e. There are six bones in the brain.   ____

f. The liver is near the stomach.   ____

g. There are two kidneys in the picture. ____

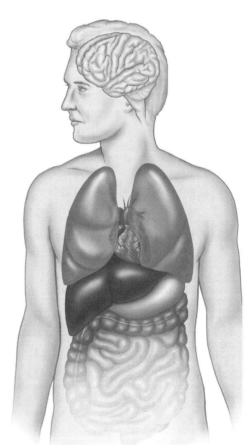

Personal Hygiene

1. **Check (✓) the words you know. Open your dictionary. Find the words you don't know.**

> ### Word List: Personal Hygiene
> #### Dictionary page 108
>
> | | | |
> |---|---|---|
> | ☐ **take** a shower | ☐ **put on** sunscreen | ☐ **brush** hair |
> | ☐ **take** a bath | ☐ **wash** hair | ☐ soap |
> | ☐ **use** deodorant | ☐ **dry** hair | ☐ shampoo |

2. **Cross out the word that doesn't belong.**

   a. wash hair   dry hair   ~~soap~~   **d.** dry   bath   shower

   b. soap   sunscreen   shampoo   **e.** wash   take   dry

   c. sunscreen   brush   deodorant

3. **Look at the pictures. Complete the sentences. Use the words in the box.**

shampoo	soap	~~take~~	use	dry	wash

   a. Every morning I ___take___ a shower. I wash my face and body with _____.

   b. I _____ my hair. I use my favourite _____.

   c. I _____ my hair.

   d. I _____ deodorant. Then I get dressed.

4. Check (✓) the things you do and the things you use every day.
Use your dictionary for help.

> ### Word List: Personal Hygiene
> #### Dictionary page 109
>
> ☐ **brush** teeth   ☐ **cut** nails   ☐ dental floss
>
> ☐ **floss** teeth   ☐ toothbrush   ☐ razor
>
> ☐ **shave**   ☐ toothpaste   ☐ shaving cream

5. Match the words with the pictures.

1.   2.   3.    4.

_2_ **a.** toothbrush   ___ **c.** dental floss   ___ **e.** shaving cream

___ **b.** toothpaste   ___ **d.** razor

6. Complete the puzzle.

ACROSS

1. ___ your nails.

5. Use a ___ with shaving cream.

6. Use ___ with a toothbrush.

DOWN

1. Use shaving ___.

2. ___ your teeth.

3. Use dental ___.

4. Use a razor to ___.

	¹C	U	T					
			²		³		⁴	
⁵								
⁶								

See page 282 for listening practice.   109

Symptoms and Injuries

1. **Check (✓) the words you know. Open your dictionary.
   Find the words you don't know.**

   ┌───┐
   │ **Word List: Symptoms and Injuries**   │
   │ Dictionary pages 110   │

☐ headache	☐ stomach ache	☐ fever
☐ toothache	☐ backache	☐ **feel** dizzy
☐ earache	☐ sore throat	☐ **feel** nauseous

2. **Look at the pictures. Circle the correct words.**

   a. He has a (fever)/
      toothache.

   b. He has a backache /
      an earache.

   c. He has a sore throat /
      headache.

   d. She has a sore throat /
      stomachache.

   e. He feels dizzy / nauseous.

3. **Read the appointment book. Answer the questions.**

TIME	PATIENT NAME	SYMPTOM
9:00 am	Paul Lee	sore throat
9:15 am	Sue Jones	fever/sore throat
9:30 am	Tomas Brown	stomach ache
9:45 am	Erica Ortiz	sore throat
10:00 am	Janet Young	earache/sore throat
10:15 am	Julio Ruiz	fever/nauseous/headache
10:30 am	Tim Emami	stomach ache

a. How many people have
   stomach aches? _____two_____

b. How many people feel
   nauseous? _____

c. How many people have
   stomach aches or
   headaches? _____

d. What symptom is the
   same for four
   people? _____

110   See page 283 for listening practice.

1. Check (✓) the illnesses and conditions that are common in your family.

Word List: Illnesses and Medical Conditions
Dictionary page 111

☐ cold	☐ chicken pox	☐ heart disease
☐ flu	☐ allergies	☐ diabetes
☐ ear infection	☐ asthma	☐ high blood pressure

2. Cross out the word that doesn't belong.

a.	cold	~~diabetes~~	flu
b.	high blood pressure	heart disease	allergies
c.	asthma	ear infection	diabetes
d.	heart disease	chicken pox	ear infection
e.	medical condition	diabetes	cold

3. Read the medical form. Write *T* (true) or *F* (false).

NAME:	Tom Brown				
REASON FOR VISIT TODAY:	headache, sore throat, fever, dizziness				

DO YOU HAVE:	YES	NO		YES	NO
Allergies	☐	☑	Heart disease	☐	☑
Asthma	☐	☑	High blood pressure	☑	☐
Diabetes	☑	☐			

a. Tom has asthma. _____F_____

b. Tom has two medical conditions. _____

c. Tom feels nauseous today. _____

d. Tom has a sore throat today. _____

e. Tom has diabetes. _____

Challenge Look at Tom's symptoms. What illness do you think he has?

1. Check (✓) the medication you buy sometimes. Use your dictionary for help.

> ### Word List: A Pharmacy
> Dictionary pages 112–113
>
> | | | | |
> |---|---|---|---|
> | ☐ pharmacist | ☐ over-the-counter medication | ☐ cream | ☐ eye drops |
> | ☐ prescription | | ☐ pain reliever | ☐ nasal spray |
> | ☐ prescription label | ☐ pill | ☐ antacid | ☐ inhaler |
> | ☐ prescription number | ☐ tablet | ☐ cough syrup | |
> | | ☐ capsule | | |

2. Match the words with the definitions.

_4_ **a.** pharmacist	**1.** medication for the skin
___ **b.** cream	**2.** medication for the eye
___ **c.** eye drops	**3.** medication you get from a pharmacist
___ **d.** prescription	**4.** a person who works in the pharmacy
___ **e.** nasal spray	**5.** medication for the nose

3. Look at the pictures. Circle the correct words.

a. He needs some cream / ⟨cough syrup⟩.

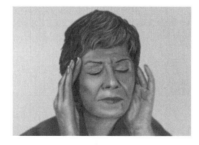

b. She needs a pain reliever / nasal spray.

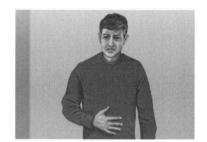

c. He needs some eye drops / antacid.

d. She's using nasal spray / tablets.

e. She needs some pills / eye drops.

f. She's using an antacid / inhaler.

4. Unscramble the words.

a. pslauesc

_____capsules_____

b. emarc

_____

c. tbleats

_____

d. gucoh psury

_____ _____

e. learhin

_____

f. phaarcistm

_____

5. Read the prescription label. Answer the questions.

a. Is this over-the-counter medication?
    No, it isn't.

b. Is the prescription for tablets?
    _____

c. What is the prescription number?
    _____

d. How many capsules does Maria take in one day?
    _____

e. How many capsules does she take in one week?
    _____

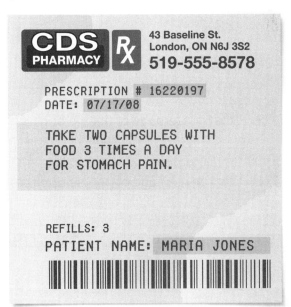

```
CDS  Rx    43 Baseline St.
PHARMACY   London, ON N6J 3S2
           519-555-8578

PRESCRIPTION # 16220197
DATE: 07/17/08

TAKE TWO CAPSULES WITH
FOOD 3 TIMES A DAY
FOR STOMACH PAIN.

REFILLS: 3
PATIENT NAME: MARIA JONES
```

Taking Care of Your Health

1. **Check (✓) the things you do when you're sick. Use your dictionary for help.**

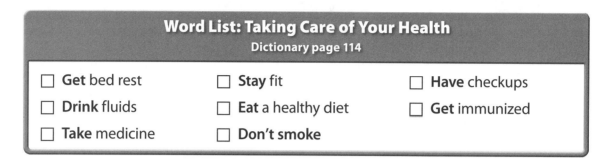

> **Word List: Taking Care of Your Health**
> Dictionary page 114
>
> ☐ **Get** bed rest   ☐ **Stay** fit   ☐ **Have** checkups
> ☐ **Drink** fluids   ☐ **Eat** a healthy diet   ☐ **Get** immunized
> ☐ **Take** medicine   ☐ **Don't smoke**

2. **Match the words with the sentences.**

   _3_ **a.** Get   **1.** checkups

   ___ **b.** Take   **2.** a healthy diet

   ___ **c.** Eat   **3.** immunized

   ___ **d.** Have   **4.** fit

   ___ **e.** Stay   **5.** fluids

   ___ **f.** Drink   **6.** medicine

3. **Study the graph. Answer the questions.**

   a. What percentage of people stay fit?

   _22%_

   b. What percentage of people eat

   a healthy diet? _____

   c. What percentage of people don't smoke?

   _____

   d. What percentage of people don't stay fit?

   _____

   e. What percentage of people stay fit, eat a
   healthy diet, and don't smoke?

   _____

Do People in Canada Take Care of Their Health?

	0	25%	50%	75%	100%
				76%	
	23%				
	22%				
All the above	3%				

Challenge Name one way you take care of your health every day.

114

4. Check (✓) the words you know. Open your dictionary. Find the words you don't know.

> **Word List: Taking Care of Your Health**
> **Dictionary page 115**
>
> ☐ vision problems   ☐ stress   ☐ glasses
> ☐ hearing loss   ☐ depression   ☐ hearing aid
> ☐ pain   ☐ optometrist   ☐ therapy

5. Look at the pictures. Check (✓) the correct sentences.

1. ✓ She has hearing loss.

   ☐ She needs glasses.

2. ☐ He has vision problems.

   ☐ He has back pain.

3. ☐ She's an optometrist.

   ☐ He's getting a hearing aid.

6. Read the doctor's advice. Circle the correct words.

a. The problem is depression /(stress) at work.

b. It's important to take care of your health / therapy.

c. The doctor gives three / four ideas for help.

d. One of the doctor's ideas is pain / therapy.

e. People with a lot of stress sometimes have depression / work.

> ## Health Advice by Dr. Bob
>
> **Dear Dr. Bob,**
> I have too much stress at work. I can't sleep and I feel sad all the time. What can I do to feel better?
> Stressed Out in Calgary
>
> **Dear Stressed,**
> Doctors know that stress can cause depression. You need to take care of your health now. Therapy, exercise, and a healthy diet can help.

Challenge Name another way to take care of stress and depression.

Medical Emergencies

1. **Check (✓) the words you know. Open your dictionary. Find the words you don't know.**

Word List: Medical Emergencies Dictionary pages 116		
☐ ambulance	☐ **have** a heart attack	☐ **choke**
☐ paramedic	☐ **burn**	☐ **bleed**
☐ **be** hurt	☐ **drown**	☐ **break** a bone

2. **Complete the words. Write the letters.**

    a. p _a_ ra _m_ e _d_ i c   **d.** c __ o __ __

    b. b e h __ __ t   **e.** __ __ b __ l a n __ e

    c. b __ __ n   **f.** b __ __ a __ a __ o n __

3. **Look at the picture. Write _T_ (true) or _F_ (false).**

    a. The girl is bleeding.   _T_

    b. Two people are hurt.   ___

    c. The paramedics are in the ambulance.   ___

    d. One paramedic is having a heart attack. ___

    e. The girl is choking.   ___

    f. One paramedic is drowning.   ___

116

1. Check (✓) the things you have at home. Use your dictionary for help.

> **Word List: First Aid**
> Dictionary page 117
>
> ☐ first aid kit   ☐ tweezers   ☐ gauze   ☐ stitches
> ☐ first aid manual   ☐ adhesive bandage   ☐ ice pack   ☐ CPR

2. Look at the pictures. Unscramble the sentences.

 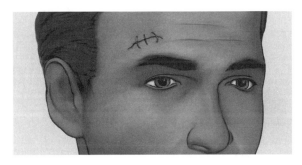

a. _She has a first aid kit._   b. _____
first aid   kit.   a   has   She   has   He   stitches.   three

c. _____   d. _____
woman   giving   The   CPR.   is   ambulance.   in   first aid   The   is
                                        manual   the

3. Look at the picture. Write the numbers.

1. first aid manual
2. tweezers
3. adhesive bandages
4. ice pack
5. ~~gauze~~
6. sterile tape

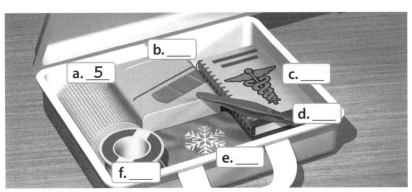

a. _5_   b. ____   c. ____   d. ____   e. ____   f. ____

117

1. **Check (✓) the words you know. Open your dictionary. Find the words you don't know.**

Word List: Medical Care
Dictionary page 118

☐ appointment	☐ doctor	☐ **check** (your) blood pressure
☐ health card	☐ patient	☐ **take** (your) temperature
☐ health history form	☐ nurse	☐ **draw** blood

2. **Complete the pictures. Use all the words in the Word List.**

Procedures	People	Things
a. *check your blood pressure*	d.	g.
b.	e.	h.
c.	f.	i.

3. **Look at the pictures. Put the sentences in order (1–6).**

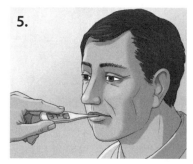

____ The nurse checks his blood pressure.

__1__ He makes an appointment to see the doctor.

____ He completes a health history form.

____ The nurse takes his temperature.

____ He talks to the doctor.

____ He shows his health insurance card.

 See page 286 for listening practice.

1. Check (✓) the words you know. Open your dictionary. Find the words you don't know.

> ### Word List: Dental Care
> #### Dictionary page 119
>
> | | | |
> |---|---|---|
> | ☐ dentist | ☐ filling | ☐ **clean** teeth |
> | ☐ dental hygienist | ☐ crown | ☐ **take** X-rays |
> | ☐ cavity | ☐ gum disease | ☐ **fill** a cavity |

2. Cross out the word that doesn't belong.

a. take X-rays   clean teeth   ~~gum disease~~

b. crown   dentist   dental hygienist

c. cavity   dentist   gum disease

d. crown   filling   clean teeth

e. fill a cavity   dental hygienist   clean teeth

3. Look at the pictures. Check (✓) the correct sentences.

 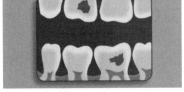 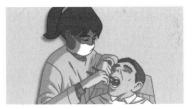

a. ☐ The dentist is filling a cavity.

✓ The patient is getting a new crown.

b. ☐ This is gum disease.

☐ There are two cavities.

c. ☐ She's a hygienist.

☐ It's a new crown.

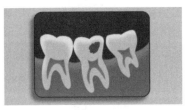 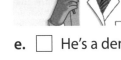 

d. ☐ The patient needs a filling.

☐ The patient needs an X-ray.

e. ☐ He's a dentist.

☐ He's taking X-rays.

f. ☐ She has gum disease.

☐ She receives good dental care.

Hospital

1. **Check (✓) the doctors you go to. Use your dictionary for help.**

> **Word List: Hospital**
> **Dictionary page 120**
>
> ☐ internist   ☐ pediatrician   ☐ nursing assistant
> ☐ obstetrician   ☐ psychiatrist   ☐ orderly
> ☐ cardiologist   ☐ nurse

2. **Match the words with the definitions.**

_5_ **a.** psychiatrist
___ **b.** nurse
___ **c.** internist
___ **d.** pediatrician
___ **e.** cardiologist
___ **f.** obstetrician

1. a doctor for children
2. a doctor for heart problems
3. a doctor for pregnant women
4. a doctor for general problems
5. a doctor for mental illnesses
6. a person who works with doctors to care for patients

3. **Look at the pictures. Read the sentences. Number the people.**

_2_ **a.**    ___ **b.**    ___ **c.**

___ **d.**    ___ **e.**    ___ **f.**

1. Dr. Aziz is a pediatrician.
2. Tanya Orloff is a nursing assistant.
3. Dr. Kumar is a cardiologist.
4. Dr. Chen is an obstetrician.
5. Ms Hart is a nurse.
6. Luis Ramos is an orderly.

4. Check (✓) the things in a hospital room. Use your dictionary for help.

> **Word List: Hospital**
> **Dictionary page 121**
>
> ☐ patient ☐ hospital bed ☐ call button
> ☐ hospital gown ☐ medical chart ☐ blood work
> ☐ medication ☐ IV

5. Label the pictures. Use the words in the box.

> call button IV hospital bed ~~medical chart~~ patient blood work

a. _medical chart_

b. _____

c. _____

d. _____

e. _____

f. _____

6. Read the story. Circle the correct words.

a. Kim is in the (hospital) / patient.

b. She puts on a hospital gown / call button.

c. The nurse gives Kim some hospital / medication.

d. He reads Kim's hospital bed / medical chart.

e. Kim needs some blood work / call button.

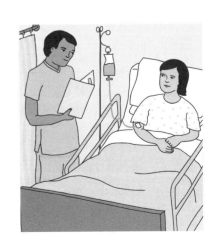

See page 287 for listening practice.

1. Check (✓) the words you know. Open your dictionary. Find the words you don't know.

Word List: A Health Fair
Dictionary pages 122–123

- ☐ low-cost exam
- ☐ acupuncture
- ☐ booth
- ☐ yoga

- ☐ aerobic exercise
- ☐ demonstration
- ☐ sugar-free

- ☐ nutrition label
- ☐ **check** (your) pulse
- ☐ **give** a lecture

---

2. Match the words with the pictures.

_8_ **a.** booth

___ **b.** give a lecture

___ **c.** medical exam

___ **d.** aerobic exercise

___ **e.** nutrition label

___ **f.** yoga

___ **g.** acupuncture

___ **h.** check…pulse

1.

2.

3.

4.

5.

6.

7.

8.

3. Look at the pictures. Circle the correct words.

a. Pam is at the health fair / exam.

b. There are many nutrition labels / booths to visit.

c. First, she goes to the exercise demonstration / lecture about nutrition labels / yoga.

d. Pam wants to get more sugar-free food / exercise.

e. She watches the yoga / acupuncture demonstration.

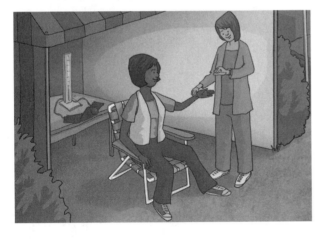

f. Pam eats a healthy lunch. Then she gets a medical exam / nutrition label.

g. A nurse takes Pam's blood pressure and booth / pulse.

h. Pam is having a great day at the aerobic exercise / health fair.

4. What about you? How often do you do these healthy things?

	Every Week	Every Year	Never
I read nutrition labels . . .			
I have a medical exam . . .			
I do aerobic exercises . . .			

1. Check (✓) the places you go every week.

Word List: Downtown
Dictionary pages 124–125

☐ parking garage   ☐ police station   ☐ post office

☐ office building   ☐ bus station   ☐ fire station

☐ hotel   ☐ city hall   ☐ courthouse

☐ driver licensing office   ☐ hospital   ☐ restaurant

☐ bank   ☐ gas station   ☐ library

2. Match the words.

_2_ **a.** city   **1.** garage

___ **b.** post   **2.** hall

___ **c.** bus   **3.** licensing office

___ **d.** parking   **4.** station

___ **e.** office   **5.** office

___ **f.** driver   **6.** building

3. Read the sentences. Write _T_ (true) or _F_ (false).

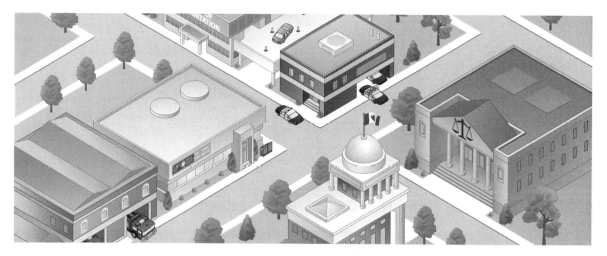

a. There are mailboxes at the post office. _T_

b. There are police cars at the fire station. ___

c. You can take a driving test at the driver licensing office. ___

d. There are police cars at the police station. ___

e. You can sleep at the courthouse. ___

f. You can buy gas at city hall. ___

4. Complete the sentences. Use the words in the box.

hospital	library	restaurant	~~parking garage~~
gas station	hotel	post office	office building

a. Roberto wants to park his car.
He's looking for a _parking garage_.

b. Mrs. Smith is going to have a baby.
She's going to the _____.

c. Mr. Tran is visiting Montreal.
He's going to a _____.

d. Fran needs stamps.
She's at the _____.

e. Rosa has a business meeting. She's
going to an _____.

f. Bill needs gas for his car.
He's at the _____.

g. Elda is hungry.
She's at the _____.

h. Mr. Patel wants some new books.
He's going to the _____.

5. Think about where you live. Answer the questions.

a. Is there a bank downtown? _____

b. Is there a library downtown? _____

c. Do you like to go downtown? _____

1. **Check (✓) the places you like. Look in your dictionary for help.**

> ### Word List: City Streets
> Dictionary pages 126–127
>
> ☐ stadium   ☐ school   ☐ synagogue
>
> ☐ factory   ☐ gym   ☐ community college
>
> ☐ mosque   ☐ coffee shop   ☐ supermarket
>
> ☐ movie theatre   ☐ motel   ☐ bakery
>
> ☐ shopping mall   ☐ church

2. **Cross out the word that doesn't belong.**

   a. ~~motel~~   coffee shop   bakery

   b. school   shopping mall   community college

   c. movie theatre   stadium   factory

   d. supermarket   motel   bakery

   e. gym   church   synagogue

3. **Label the picture. Use the words in the box.**

   > gym   motel   coffee shop   community college   school   ~~supermarket~~

a. *supermarket*

b. _____

c. _____

d. _____

e. _____

f. _____

4. Look at the pictures. Check (✓) the correct sentences.

a. ✓ They're at the movie theatre.

☐ They're at the stadium.

b. ☐ He's at school.

☐ He's at the gym.

c. ☐ They're at the coffee shop.

☐ They're at the mall.

d. ☐ The mosque is large.

☐ The church is small.

e. ☐ She works at the motel.

☐ She works at the supermarket.

f. ☐ He's at the factory.

☐ He's at the bakery.

5. Study the bus schedule. Answer the questions. Write *yes* or *no*.

a. Tim is at the mall. He's going to the stadium.
Can he take this bus? _____

b. Sharon lives on Main Street. She has a class
at 12:15. Can she take this bus? _____

c. It's 12:00. Mary is at the college.
She wants to see a movie at 12:30.
Can she take this bus? _____

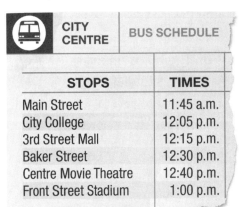

CITY CENTRE	BUS SCHEDULE	
STOPS	**TIMES**	
Main Street	11:45 a.m.	
City College	12:05 p.m.	
3rd Street Mall	12:15 p.m.	
Baker Street	12:30 p.m.	
Centre Movie Theatre	12:40 p.m.	
Front Street Stadium	1:00 p.m.	

See page 288 for listening practice.

1. **Check (✓) the people, places, and things you see every day. Look in your dictionary for help.**

> ### Word List: An Intersection
> #### Dictionary pages 128–129
>
> | | | |
> |---|---|---|
> | ☐ laundromat | ☐ corner | ☐ crosswalk |
> | ☐ dry cleaners | ☐ traffic light | ☐ bus stop |
> | ☐ convenience store | ☐ bus | ☐ bike |
> | ☐ pharmacy | ☐ mailbox | ☐ sidewalk |
> | ☐ parking space | ☐ pedestrian | ☐ parking meter |

2. **Write the words in the chart. Use the words in the box.**

> | | | | |
> |---|---|---|---|
> | sidewalk | crosswalk | dry cleaners | ~~convenience store~~ |
> | intersection | parking space | pharmacy | |

Places to Go	Places for Pedestrians	Places for Cars
convenience store		

3. **What's wrong with the picture? Circle the correct words.**

a. A pedestrian /(car) is in the crosswalk.

b. The pedestrians are in the mailbox / intersection.

c. The car is in two parking meters / parking spaces.

d. The bus is on the sidewalk / in the intersection.

4. Read the sentences. Label the picture with the numbers.

1. Irma is in the crosswalk.

2. Hari is on the sidewalk.

3. Joe is on the corner of Main and Green Street.

4. Fred is in front of the laundromat.

5. Mary is at the parking meter.

6. Bella is at the bus stop.

5. Look at the chart. Answer the questions.

a. How many people drive a car? __45__ %

b. How many people ride the bus? ____%

c. How many people are pedestrians? ____%

d. How many people aren't pedestrians? ____%

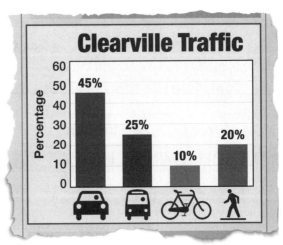

Challenge Do you think it's easy or difficult to find a parking space in Clearville?

See page 289 for listening practice.

1. Check (✓) the places you like to shop. Look in your dictionary for help.

> ### Word List: A Mall
> #### Dictionary pages 130–131
>
> | | | |
> |---|---|---|
> | ☐ music store | ☐ pet store | ☐ food court |
> | ☐ jewellery store | ☐ card store | ☐ hair salon |
> | ☐ nail salon | ☐ optician | ☐ elevator |
> | ☐ bookstore | ☐ shoe store | ☐ escalator |
> | ☐ toy store | ☐ department store | ☐ directory |

2. Match the words with the pictures.

1.
2.
3.
4.
5.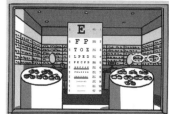
6.

_4_ **a.** bookstore

___ **c.** music store

___ **e.** department store

___ **b.** optician

___ **d.** hair salon

___ **f.** jewellery store

3. Complete the sentences. Use the words in the box.

elevator	toy store	~~directory~~	shoe store	card store

a. Tan is looking for the pet store. He needs a _____ _directory_ _____.

b. Marta wants new shoes. She's going to the _____.

c. Frank wants to go to the second floor. He needs an _____.

d. Billy wants a new ball. He's looking for the _____.

e. Diana is buying a birthday card for her friend. She's at the _____.

4. Study the map and the directory. Write _T_ (true) or _F_ (false).

a. There's a department store in the mall.   _T_

b. There's an optician in the mall.   ——

c. The directory shows six stores.   ——

d. The food court is next to the nail salon.   ——

e. There's an escalator near the food court.   ——

f. Hair Today is a toy store.   ——

g. Tammi's is a card store.   ——

h. The music store is next to the bookstore.   ——

5. What about you? Answer the questions.

a. Do you like to shop at the mall?   _____

b. Is there a mall near your home?   _____

c. Name three kinds of stores you like.   _____

The Bank

1. **Check (✓) the words you know. Look in your dictionary. Find the words you don't know.**

> ### Word List: The Bank
> #### Dictionary page 132
>
> ☐ teller ☐ chequing account number ☐ balance
> ☐ customer ☐ ATM card ☐ **cash** a cheque
> ☐ chequebook ☐ bank statement ☐ **make** a deposit

2. **Look at the pictures. Write _T_ (true) or _F_ (false).**

Town Bank
MONTHLY STATEMENT
Account: Chequing
Account Number: 746555 001
Balance: $548.79

a. It's a bank statement. _T_

b. The chequing account number is 746555 001. ____

c. The balance is $465.55. ____

d. The customer is cashing a cheque. ____

e. The customer has an ATM card. ____

f. The customer is making a deposit. ____

g. They're new customers. ____

h. They're getting a chequebook. ____

i. They're talking to a teller. ____

3. **Complete the story. Use the words in the box.**

> ~~customer~~ teller deposit ATM card balance

Ingrid is a __customer__ at Town Bank. She makes a _____ every Friday.
a.   b.

She talks to a _____ or she uses her _____. Her _____ is $1,200.00.
c.   d.   e.

1. **Check (✓) the words you know. Look in your dictionary. Find the words you don't know.**

> **Word List: The Library**
> Dictionary page 133
>
> ☐ **get** a library card   ☐ **return** a book   ☐ picture book
> ☐ **look for** a book   ☐ **pay** a late fine   ☐ title
> ☐ **check out** a book   ☐ library clerk   ☐ author

2. **Label the pictures with the numbers.**

___6___ **a.**    ___ **b.**    ___ **c.**

___ **d.**    ___ **e.**    ___ **f.**

1. Talk to a library clerk.   3. Get a library card.   5. Look for a book.
2. Return a book.   4. Pay a late fine.   6. Check out a book.

3. **Look at the book. Answer the questions.**

a. What is the title?   _____

b. Who is the author?   _____

c. What kind of book is it?   _____

1. **Check (✓) the words you know. Look in your dictionary. Find the words you don't know.**

   Word List: The Post Office
   Dictionary pages 134–135

   ☐ postal clerk   ☐ package   ☐ stamp
   ☐ letter   ☐ book of stamps   ☐ **Address** the envelope
   ☐ envelope   ☐ letter carrier   ☐ **Put on** a stamp
   ☐ greeting card   ☐ return address   ☐ **Mail** the card
   ☐ postcard   ☐ mailing address

2. **Cross out the word that doesn't belong.**

   a. letter carrier   ~~stamp~~   postal clerk

   b. return address   mailing address   book of stamps

   c. post office   package   letter

   d. greeting card   postcard   postal clerk

   e. Address the envelope. greeting card   Put on a stamp.

3. **Complete the story. Use the words in the box.**

   | address | ~~greeting~~ | envelope | stamp |
   | post office | return | mails | book |

   a. Mira buys a __greeting__ card at the card shop.

   b. She puts the card in an _____.

   c. She writes the mailing _____ and the _____ address on the envelope.

   d. Then she buys a _____ of stamps at the _____.

   e. She puts a _____ on the envelope.

   f. She _____ the card.

4. Look at the picture. Write *T* (true) or *F* (false).

a. Luz is a postal clerk. __T__

b. The customer is mailing an envelope. _____

c. Larry is a postal clerk. _____

d. Larry carries cards, letters, postcards, and packages. _____

e. You can buy stamps for postcards at the post office. _____

f. You can buy stamps for letters at the post office. _____

5. Read the information. Complete the envelope.

Kainda Wangai is mailing the letter. Her address is 22 Green Street, Toronto, ON M5V 2G1.

The letter is going to Matu Wangai. His address is 919 Glad Street, Red Deer, AB T4P 3A0.

a. Write Kainda's address on the envelope.

b. Write Matu's address on the envelope.

c. Draw a stamp on the envelope.

1. Check (✓) the things you get at the Driver Licensing Office.
Look in your dictionary for help.

> ### Word List: Driver Licensing Office
> #### Dictionary page 136
>
> ☐ licensing clerk ☐ window ☐ driver's licence number
>
> ☐ photo ☐ proof of insurance ☐ licence plate
>
> ☐ signature ☐ driver's licence ☐ registration sticker
>
> ☐ vision exam

2. Label the pictures with the numbers.

<u>3</u> **a.**  **b.** ___  **c.** ___

d. ___  **e.** ___  **f.** ___ *Jane Doe*

1. registration sticker **3.** licence plate **5.** driver's licence

2. driver's licence number **4.** photo **6.** signature

3. Look at the picture. Circle the correct words.

a. Mario is at the photo / <u>Driver Licensing Office</u>.

b. He needs a new <u>driver's licence</u> / window.

c. He goes to the <u>window</u> / stickers.

d. He talks to a registration / <u>clerk</u>.

e. He gets a proof of insurance / <u>vision exam</u>.

f. The clerk takes his licence number / <u>photo</u>
and gets his <u>signature</u> / licence plate.

DRIVER LICENSING OFFICE

4. Put the steps in order (1-5). Look in your dictionary for help.

Word List: Driver Licensing Office
Dictionary page 137

☐ **Get** your licence   ☐ **Pay** the application fee   ☐ **Take** a written test

☐ **Pass** a driving test   ☐ **Take** a driver education and training course

---

5. Look at the pictures. Complete the story. Use the words in the box.

driver's licence	written test	proof of insurance
driving test	photo	application fee

a. Elena is getting her _driver's licence_.

b. She pays the _____.

c. She takes a _____.

d. She shows _____.

e. She passes the _____.

f. She takes a _____.

See page 292 for listening practice.

1. Check (✓) the words you know. Look in your dictionary. Find the words you don't know.

Word List: Government and Military Service
Dictionary page 138

- ☐ House of Commons
- ☐ prime minister
- ☐ Parliament of Canada
- ☐ senator
- ☐ Supreme Court of Canada
- ☐ judges
- ☐ army
- ☐ navy
- ☐ air force

2. Take the test. Fill in the answers.

Social Studies paper one
General Quiz

Name: _____

Date: _____

School: _____

YOUR SCORE

Correct Answers

Wrong Answers

1. What are the three branches of the military?
   - a) cabinet, Senate, House of Commons
   - (army, navy, air force)

2. Who is part of the Supreme Court of Canada?
   - a) senators
   - b) the chief justice

3. Where do members of parliament work?
   - a) in the House of Commons
   - b) on the Supreme Court of Canada

4. What is NOT part of Canada's military?
   - a) the Navy
   - b) members of parliament

5. Who works in Canadian Parliament?
   - a) the air force
   - b) the prime minister

6. Which sentence is true?
   - a) The air force works with airplanes.
   - b) The army works with the chief justice.

3. Check (✓) the words you know. Look in your dictionary. Find the words you don't know.

> ## Word List: Government and Military Service
> ### Dictionary page 139
>
> **Provincial Government**
> ☐ premier
> ☐ provincial capital
> ☐ Legislature
>
> **City Government**
> ☐ mayor
> ☐ city council
> ☐ city councillor

4. Complete the words. Write the letters.

a. m _a_ y _o_ r

b. p __ __ m __ e r

c. ci __ __   c __ __ n c __ __

d. L __ __ is __ a t u r e

e. __ r o __ i n c __ __ l   c __ p i __ a l

f. c __ __ y   c __ u n __ i __ __ o r

5. Complete the sentences. Use the words in the box.

> city   city council   provincial capital   premier   city councillor   ~~government~~

a. The premier is part of the provincial ____government____.

b. The premier lives and works in the _____.

c. The House of Assembly and the _____ work together.

d. The mayor is part of _____ government.

e. The mayor works with the _____.

f. Every _____ on the city council is important.

Challenge Who is the leader of your country? Who is the mayor of your city?

Civic Rights and Responsibilities

1. **Check (✓) your rights and responsibilities. Look in your dictionary for help.**

> ## Word List: Civic Rights and Responsibilities
> ### Dictionary page 140
>
> | Responsibilities | Citizenship Requirements | Rights |
> |---|---|---|
> | ☐ **vote** in elections | ☐ **live** in Canada for 3 of the last 4 years | ☐ **freedom** of thought, belief, opinion, and expression |
> | ☐ **help** others in the community | ☐ **take** a citizenship test | ☐ **freedom** of conscience and religion |
> | ☐ **obey** Canada's laws | | ☐ **freedom** of association |
> | ☐ **care** for and **protect** our heritage and environment | | |

2. **Match the words.**

   _3_ **a.** help   **1.** a citizenship test

   ___ **b.** live   **2.** Canada's laws

   ___ **c.** take   **3.** others in the community

   ___ **d.** obey   **4.** and protect our heritage and environment

   ___ **e.** care for   **5.** in Canada for 3 of the last 4 years

3. **Look at the pictures. Check the correct sentences.**

a.

b.

   ✓ They have freedom of religion.
   ☐ They have the right to peaceful assembly.

   ☐ He's going to vote.
   ☐ He's going to eliminate discrimination and injustice.

c.

d.

   ☐ She's taking a citizenship test.

   ☐ She has the right to freedom of thought, belief, opinion, and expression.

   ☐ He's going to care for and protect our heritage and environment.

   ☐ He has the right to conscience and religion.

  See page 294 for listening practice.

1. Check (✓) the words you know. Look in your dictionary. Find the words you don't know.

Word List: The Legal System
Dictionary page 141

☐ police officer   ☐ jury   ☐ **hire** a lawyer

☐ defendant   ☐ witness   ☐ **go** to jail

☐ judge   ☐ **arrest** a suspect   ☐ **be** released

---

2. Label the pictures. Use the words in the box.

| jury | ~~judge~~ | witness | lawyer | jail | police officer |

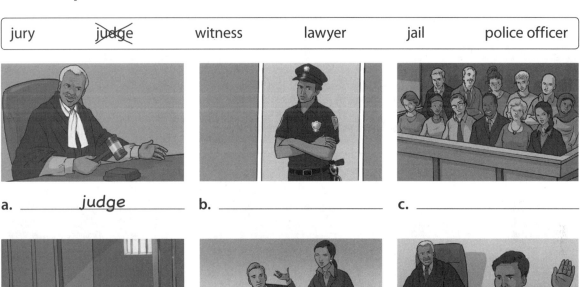

a. _____judge_____   b. _____   c. _____

d. _____   e. _____   f. _____

3. Read the sentences. Write *T* (true) or *F* (false).

a. A police officer can arrest a suspect.   _T_

b. A defendant can hire a lawyer.   ___

c. A suspect can arrest a police officer.   ___

d. A defendant can go to jail or be released.   ___

e. A defendant can hire a judge.

f. A judge can talk to a lawyer.   ___

**1. Check (✓) the words you know. Look in your dictionary.
Find the words you don't know.**

> ### Word List: Crime
> #### Dictionary page 142
>
> ☐ vandalism   ☐ shoplifting   ☐ mugging
>
> ☐ burglary   ☐ identity theft   ☐ murder
>
> ☐ drunk driving   ☐ victim   ☐ gun

2. Unscramble the words.

a. ugn   g _u_ _n_

b. durmer   m ___ r ___ ___ r

c. tmivic   ___ ___ c ___ ___ m

d. gugingm   ___ ___ g g ___ ___ g

e. largybur   b ___ ___ g ___ ___ ___ y

f. nkrud divirng   ___ r ___ ___ k d ___ ___ v ___ ___ ___

3. Label the pictures. Use the words in the box.

> shoplifting   vandalism   ~~identity theft~~   burglary   mugging   murder

a. _identity theft_

b. _____

c. _____

d. _____

e. _____

f. _____

1. Check (✓) the things you do to be safe. Look in your dictionary for help.

> **Word List: Public Safety**
> Dictionary page 143
>
> ☐ **Walk** with a friend   ☐ **Lock** your doors   ☐ **Report** crimes to the police
> ☐ **Protect** your purse   ☐ Don't **drink** and   ☐ **Join** a neighbourhood watch
>   or wallet   **drive**

2. Unscramble the sentences.

a. your Lock doors.   _Lock your doors._

b. friend. a Walk with   _____

c. your Protect purse.   _____

d. watch. a neighbourhood Join   _____

e. crimes the Report to police.   _____

3. Look at the story. Put the sentences in order (1–6).

1.

2.

3.

4.

5.

> I need to report
> a crime.

6.

> Neighbourhood
> Watch Meeting
> 7:00–8:30

____ This evening, they see a problem.   ____ They walk together in the evening.

_1_ Lidia and Carla lock their doors.   ____ They join a neighbourhood watch.

____ They report the crime to the police.   ____ They know it's a crime to drink and drive.

Emergencies and Natural Disasters

1. **Check (✓) the emergencies and disasters. Look in your dictionary for help.**

> ### Word List: Emergencies and Natural Disasters
> #### Dictionary page 144
>
> ☐ lost child ☐ airplane crash ☐ earthquake ☐ firefighter
>
> ☐ car accident ☐ explosion ☐ fire ☐ fire truck

2. **Cross out the word that doesn't belong.**

   a. car accident ~~earthquake~~ airplane crash

   b. explosion fire lost child

   c. earthquake firefighter fire truck

   d. earthquake natural disaster car accident

   e. fire truck firefighter crash

3. **Look at the pictures. Complete the story. Use the words in the box.**

   fire ~~firefighters~~ fire truck lost child explosion

   a. Police officers and _____firefighters_____ fight a _____ .

   b. An _____ started the fire at 7:00 p.m.

   c. The first _____ arrived at 7:06.

   d. Officer Tim Juarez helps a _____ find her family.

Challenge Do the pictures show an emergency, a natural disaster, or both?

144

4. Check (✓) the disasters that happen in your country. Look in your dictionary for help.

Word List: Emergencies and Natural Disasters
Dictionary page 145

☐ drought　　☐ blizzard　　☐ tornado　　☐ flood

☐ famine　　☐ hurricane　　☐ tsunami

5. Match the words with the same idea.

_4_ **a.** hurricane　　　　**1.** a lot of snow

___ **b.** famine　　　　**2.** too much water

___ **c.** drought　　　　**3.** no rain

___ **d.** flood　　　　**4.** wind and rain

___ **e.** blizzard　　　　**5.** no food

6. Study the map. Write _T_ (true) or _F_ (false).

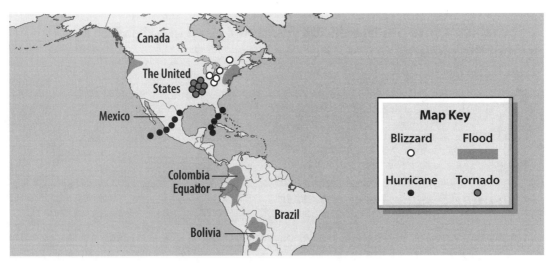

a. There are hurricanes in Brazil and Colombia.　　　　_F_

b. There are blizzards in Canada and the U.S.　　　　___

c. There are floods in Bolivia.　　　　___

d. There are hurricanes, tornadoes, and floods in the United States.　___

e. There are blizzards in Mexico.　　　　___

f. There are hurricanes in Canada.　　　　___

Challenge Name a natural disaster that happened this year.

Emergency Procedures

1. **Check (✓) the things you have at home. Look in your dictionary for help.**

    > **Word List: Emergency Procedures**
    > Dictionary page 146
    >
    > ☐ **Make** a disaster kit.   ☐ can opener   ☐ flashlight
    > ☐ warm clothes   ☐ canned food   ☐ batteries
    > ☐ blankets   ☐ bottled water ☐ first aid kit

2. **What do you need in a disaster kit? Match the words.**

    _2_ **a.** first aid   1. clothes

    ____ **b.** canned   2. kit

    ____ **c.** bottled   3. opener

    ____ **d.** warm   4. food

    ____ **e.** can   5. water

3. **Look at the list. Cross out the things you don't need in a disaster kit. Then label the picture.**

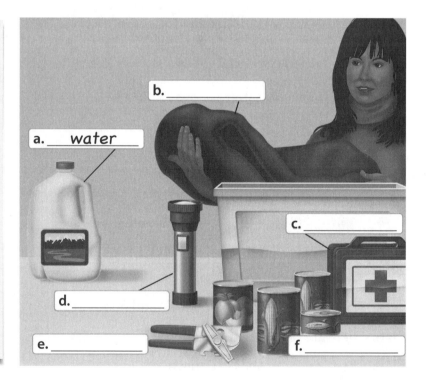

blanket
water
~~soda~~
flashlight
sandwiches
canned food
first aid kit
can opener
CD player
new shoes

a. ___water___
b. _____
c. _____
d. _____
e. _____
f. _____

Challenge Name three other things you need in a disaster kit.

4. Check (✓) the things you know how to do. Look in your dictionary for help.

> **Word List: Emergency Procedures**
> **Dictionary page 147**
>
> ☐ **Watch** the weather ☐ **Remain** calm ☐ **Clean up** debris
> ☐ **Pay attention** to warnings ☐ **Follow** directions ☐ **Inspect** utilities

5. Unscramble the sentences.

a. watch the They weather.   _They watch the weather._

b. calm. They remain   _____

c. attention to warnings. pay They   _____

d. up debris. the They clean   _____

e. the inspect They utilities.   _____

6. Look at the pictures. Circle the correct words.

Tornado Warning. Seek shelter.

a. Sue is watching the (weather) / debris.

b. Saleem is <u>inspecting / paying attention</u> to the radio.

c. The <u>warnings / utilities</u> say to seek shelter.

d. The family remains <u>upset / calm</u>.

e. They follow <u>directions / attention</u>.

f. They go home later and <u>watch / clean up</u> the debris.

g. They inspect the <u>debris / utilities</u>. Everything is fine.

See page 296 for listening practice.

Community Cleanup

1. Check (✓) the words you know. Look in your dictionary. Find the words you don't know.

> **Word List: Community Cleanup**
> Dictionary pages 148–149
>
> ☐ graffiti ☐ hardware store ☐ **give** a speech
> ☐ litter ☐ petition ☐ **applaud**
> ☐ streetlight ☐ **change**

2. Match the words with the pictures.

_5_ **a.** 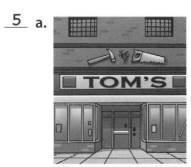 ___ **b.**  ___ **c.**

___ **d.**  ___ **e.**  ___ **f.**

1. litter 3. petition 5. ~~hardware store~~
2. graffiti 4. give a speech 6. applaud

3. Unscramble the sentences.

a. on There's the graffiti store. hardware _There's graffiti on the hardware store._

b. this street. litter on There's _____

c. streetlight The broken. is _____

d. The petition. sign a people _____

e. change They Centre Street. _____

4. Look at the pictures. Complete the story. Use the words in the box.

streetlight	applaud	petition	litter	community
hardware store	speech	~~graffiti~~	change	

a. There's ___graffiti___ on the hardware store and litter on the street.

b. A _____ is broken, too.

c. Sanjay owns the _____. He wants to clean up the street.

d. Many people sign a _____.

e. They plan a _____ cleanup.

f. Many people clean up the _____.

g. Everyone works together. They _____ the street together.

h. Later they have a party. Sanjay gives a _____.

i. He says, "Thank you, everyone!" All the people _____.

5. What about you? Answer the questions.

a. Does your neighbourhood need a community cleanup? _____

b. What do you want to change in your neighbourhood? _____

Basic Transportation

1. Check (✓) the things you use for transportation. Use your dictionary for help.

> **Word List: Basic Transportation**
> Dictionary pages 150–151
>
> ☐ car ☐ truck ☐ subway station
> ☐ passenger ☐ train ☐ subway
> ☐ taxi ☐ (air)plane ☐ bus stop
> ☐ motorcycle ☐ helicopter ☐ bus
> ☐ street ☐ airport ☐ bicycle

2. Unscramble the sentences.

a. The at bus the is bus stop.   _The bus is at the bus stop._

b. subway There's station. the   _____

c. airport. is at Sam the   _____

d. driving the is Eli truck.   _____

e. is The taxi. in passenger the   _____

3. Label the picture. Use the words in the box.

| taxi | motorcycle | helicopter | ~~bicycle~~ | airplane | subway |

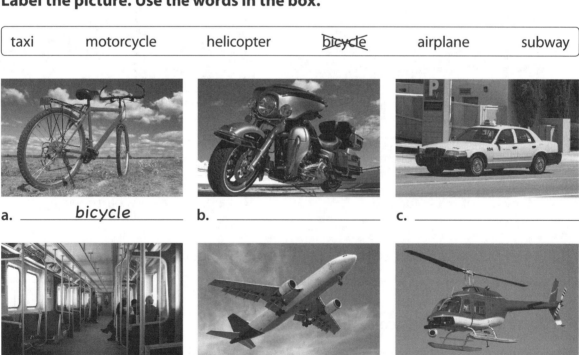

a. _____bicycle_____   b. _____   c. _____

d. _____   e. _____   f. _____

4. Study the chart. Answer the questions.

Toronto to Montreal		
Transportation	Time	Cost
Car	5 to 6 hours	$30.00
Bus	5 ½ hours	$24.00
Train	4 ½ hours	$45.50

a. Name the kinds of transportation in the chart.
_____car_____ _____ _____

b. How much does it cost to take the bus from Toronto to Montreal? _____

c. How many hours does the trip take by train? _____

d. How many hours does the trip take by car? _____

5. Study the graph. Complete the sentences.

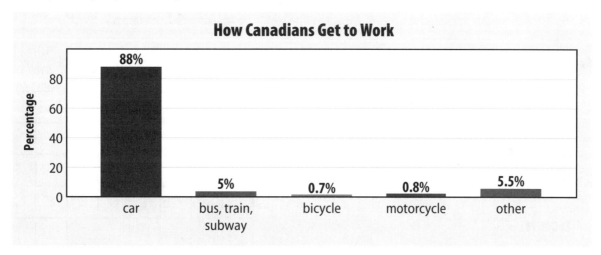

a. Eighty-eight percent of people get to work by _____car_____.

b. Five percent of people ride a train, subway, or _____.

c. Not many people ride a bicycle or a _____ to work.

d. A _____ is an example of other transportation.

6. What about you? Answer the questions.

a. Do you like airplanes? _____

b. Do you like trains? _____

c. What transportation do you usually use? _____

Public Transportation

1. **Check (✓) the words you know. Open your dictionary. Find the words you don't know.**

   ### Word List: Public Transportation
   #### Dictionary page 152

☐ fare	☐ token	☐ ticket
☐ schedule	☐ fare card	☐ one-way trip
☐ transfer	☐ ticket window	☐ round trip

2. **Complete the words. Write the letters.**

   a. t r _a_ n _s_ f _e_ _r_

   b. f __ __ e   c __ r __

   c. t __ __ k e __

   d. t __ __ __ n

   e. s __ __ e d __ l __

   f. __ n __ -w __ __   t r i p

3. **Complete the crossword puzzle.**

   ACROSS

   2. You need this for the subway.

   5. You need this to change buses.

   6. ___ trip

   DOWN

   1. It has information about bus times and stops.

   3. bus money

   4. ticket ___

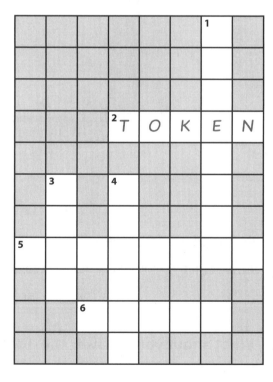

See page 297 for listening practice.

1. Check (✓) the words you know. Open your dictionary. Find the words you don't know.

> ### Word List: Prepositions of Motion
> #### Dictionary page 153
>
> ☐ **go under** the bridge   ☐ **walk down** the steps   ☐ **get on** the highway
>
> ☐ **go over** the bridge   ☐ **get into** the taxi   ☐ **get off** the highway
>
> ☐ **walk up** the steps   ☐ **get out of** the taxi   ☐ **drive through** the tunnel

2. Write the opposites. Use the words in the box.

get out of	go over	get off	~~walk down~~	walk under

a. walk up   _walk down_   **d.** get on   _____

b. go under   _____   **e.** walk over   _____

c. get into   _____

3. Read the sentences. Number the people.

1. Riku is walking down the steps.

2. Al is driving through the intersection.

3. Oscar is getting into a taxi.

4. Hansa is walking up the steps.

5. Paula is getting off the bus.

1. Check (✓) the traffic signs you see between your home and school. Use your dictionary for help.

> **Word List: Traffic Signs**
> **Dictionary page 154**
>
> ☐ stop   ☐ speed limit   ☐ yield
> ☐ do not enter   ☐ right turn only   ☐ no parking
> ☐ one way   ☐ no left turn   ☐ handicapped parking

2. Complete the signs. Use the Word List for help.

a. 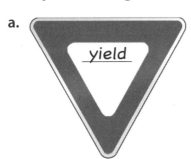 yield

b.

c.

d.

e.

f.  50

3. Look at the pictures. Write *T* (true) or *F* (false).

a. The car can turn right on Main Street.   _T_

b. First Street is one way.   ___

c. It's OK for the car to turn left onto First Street.   ___

d. There's no parking on Main Street.   ___

e. Main Street is one way.   ___

Challenge Name three traffic signs between your home and your school.

1. **Check (✓) the words you know. Open your dictionary.**
   Find the words you don't know.

Word List: Directions and Maps
Dictionary page 155

   ☐ go straight   ☐ turn left   ☐ north   ☐ south
   ☐ turn right   ☐ stop   ☐ west   ☐ east

2. **Unscramble the words.**

   a. rothn _n_ _o_ _r_ th

   b. tops   s __ __ __

   c. sewt   __ e __ __

   d. eats   __ __ __ t

   f. ouths s __ __ __ __

   g. urtn fetl __ __ __ n __ e __ __

3. **Label the picture with the numbers.**

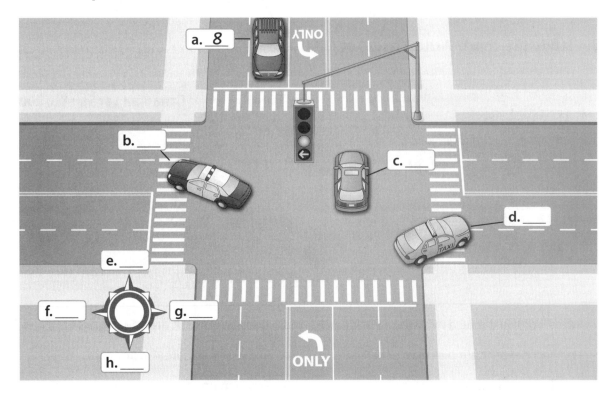

a. _8_

b. ___

c. ___

d. ___

e. ___

f. ___

g. ___

h. ___

ONLY

1. north   4. east   7. turn left
2. west   5. go straight   8. ~~stop~~
3. south   6. turn right

1. Check (✓) the cars and trucks you like. Use your dictionary for help.

Word List: Cars and Trucks
Dictionary page 156

☐ 4-door car   ☐ convertible   ☐ pickup truck
☐ 2-door car   ☐ SUV   ☐ tow truck
☐ hybrid   ☐ minivan   ☐ school bus

2. Complete the chart. Use all the words in the word list.

	Cars		Trucks		Other
a.	4-door car	e.		g.	
b.		f.		h.	
c.				i.	
d.					

3. Study the chart. Write _T_ (true) or _F_ (false).

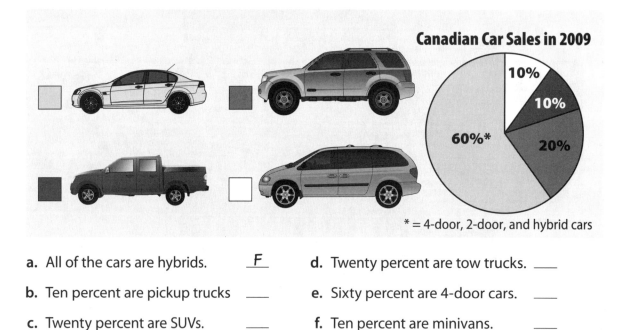

Canadian Car Sales in 2009

10%
10%
60%*
20%

* = 4-door, 2-door, and hybrid cars

a. All of the cars are hybrids.   _F_

b. Ten percent are pickup trucks ___

c. Twenty percent are SUVs.   ___

d. Twenty percent are tow trucks. ___

e. Sixty percent are 4-door cars.   ___

f. Ten percent are minivans.   ___

Challenge What do you think was the favourite colour for cars in Canada in 2009?

1. **Check (✓) the things you do before you buy a used car. Use your dictionary for help.**

> **Word List: Buying and Maintaining a Car**
> Dictionary page 157
>
> ☐ **Look at** car ads ☐ **Negotiate** a price ☐ **Fill** the tank with gas
> ☐ **Ask** the seller about the car ☐ **Get** the title from the seller ☐ **Check** the oil
> ☐ **Take** the car to a mechanic ☐ **Register** the car ☐ **Go** for an emissions test

2. **Unscramble the sentences.**

a. car ads. at Look _____*Look at car ads.*_____

b. oil. Check the _____

c. car. the Register _____

d. gas. tank with Fill the _____

e. Take a mechanic. car the to _____

3. **Look at the story. Put the sentences in order (1–6).**

1.  2.  3.

4.  5.  6.

___ He registers his car.

_1_ Eduardo is looking at a car. He asks the seller some questions.

___ He fills the tank with gas.

___ Eduardo negotiates a good price.

___ He goes for an emissions test.

___ He gets the title from the seller.

1. **Check (✓) the parts of a car that open. Use your dictionary for help.**

> ### Word List: Parts of a Car
> #### Dictionary page 158
>
> | | | |
> |---|---|---|
> | ☐ windshield | ☐ tire | ☐ gas tank |
> | ☐ (windshield) wipers | ☐ headlight | ☐ trunk |
> | ☐ hood | ☐ bumper | ☐ engine |

2. **Read the sentences. Circle the correct words.**

   a. The engine is under the (hood) / trunk.

   b. A car has four tires / bumpers.

   c. Use your gas tank / headlights at night.

   d. Use your windshield wipers / windshield in the rain.

   e. A car has two engines / bumpers.

   f. The hood / trunk is in the back of the car.

3. **Label the picture. Use the words in the box.**

hood	tire	~~windshield~~	bumper	headlight	wipers

a. _windshield_

b. _____

c. _____

d. _____

e. _____

f. _____

4. Check (✓) the things a driver uses. Use your dictionary for help.

> **Word List: Parts of a Car**
> **Dictionary page 159**
>
> ☐ steering wheel ☐ rear-view mirror ☐ seat belt
> ☐ horn ☐ hand brake ☐ back seat
> ☐ turn signal ☐ front seat

5. Match the words.

_2_ **a.** front   **1.** signal

___ **b.** turn   **2.** seat

___ **c.** seat   **3.** belt

___ **d.** steering   **4.** wheel

___ **e.** hand   **5.** mirror

___ **f.** rear-view   **6.** brake

6. Complete the sentences. Use the words in the box.

> front seat   back seat   steering wheel   seat belt   horn   ~~turn signal~~

a. Use the _____ *turn signal* _____ before you turn.

b. Use the _____ to get attention.

c. Use the _____ to steer the car.

d. The driver sits in the _____ .

e. Always wear your _____ .

f. A baby is safe in the _____ .

1. Check (✓) the words you know. Open your dictionary. Find the words you don't know.

Word List: An Airport
Dictionary pages 160–161

- ☐ ticket agent
- ☐ security screener
- ☐ gate
- ☐ flight attendant
- ☐ overhead compartment
- ☐ emergency exit
- ☐ passenger
- ☐ luggage
- ☐ e-ticket
- ☐ boarding pass
- ☐ **Check in** electronically
- ☐ **Check** your bags
- ☐ **Go through** security
- ☐ **Board** the plane
- ☐ **Take off**
- ☐ **Land**

2. Unscramble the sentences.

a. your here. Check bags   _Check your bags here._

b. plane. the Board   _____

c. plane The taking off. is   _____

d. at The plane 3:00. lands   _____

e. need to We check electronically in.   _____

f. go security. through passengers All   _____

3. Match the words with the definitions.

_2_ **a.** flight attendant

___ **b.** ticket agent

___ **c.** overhead compartment

___ **d.** e-ticket

___ **e.** gate

___ **f.** security screener

1. a ticket you buy on the Internet

2. person who works on an airplane

3. someone who works at airport security

4. someone who sells tickets

5. a place to put your luggage

6. you board the plane here

4. Look at the pictures. Circle the correct words.

a. Gloria is at the (airport)/ emergency exit.

b. She has an e-ticket / airplane.

c. She doesn't need a boarding pass / ticket agent.

d. She's checking in electronically / going through security at a computer.

e. She's going through security / boarding the plane.

f. The flight attendant / security screener is checking her boarding pass.

g. She's putting her luggage in the emergency exit / overhead compartment.

h. She's listening to the passenger / flight attendant.

i. Soon the airplane will land / take off.

5. How much do you like these jobs? Number the jobs 1–3 (1 = the job you like the best).

____ ticket agent

____ security screener

____ flight attendant

See page 299 for listening practice.

1. Check (✓) the words you know. Open your dictionary.
Find the words you don't know.

> **Word List: Taking a Trip**
> Dictionary pages 162–163
>
> ☐ starting point ☐ destination ☐ **break down**
> ☐ scenery ☐ **pack** ☐ **run out** of gas
> ☐ gas station attendant ☐ **get** lost ☐ **have** a flat tire
> ☐ auto club card ☐ **get** a speeding ticket

2. Match the words with the pictures.

1.
2.
3.
4.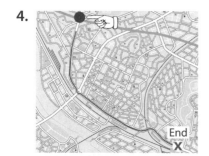
5.
6.
7.
8.
9.

__4__ **a.** starting point   ___ **d.** flat tire   ___ **g.** gas station attendant

___ **b.** scenery   ___ **e.** break down   ___ **h.** get lost

___ **c.** auto club card   ___ **f.** get a speeding ticket   ___ **i.** pack

3. Look at the pictures. Circle the correct words.

a. Paul and Sue take a <u>car</u> /(<u>trip</u>) every year. This year they're going to Vancouver.

b. First they <u>reach</u> / <u>pack</u> the car.

c. Paul always brings his <u>attendant</u> / <u>auto club card</u>.

d. On the first day of the trip, the car gets a <u>flat tire</u> / <u>speeding ticket</u>.

e. They stop at a <u>gas station</u> / <u>destination</u>.

f. A <u>speeding ticket</u> / <u>gas station attendant</u> helps them.

g. The next day they <u>run out of gas</u> / <u>reach their destination</u>.

h. The <u>scenery</u> / <u>auto club</u> is beautiful.

i. They have a great <u>trip</u> / <u>speeding ticket</u>.

4. What about you? Answer the questions. Write *Yes, I do* or *No, I don't*.

a. Do you like to take car trips? _____ .

b. Do you have an auto club card? _____ .

c. Do you usually pack too many things when you take a trip? _____ .

163

1. Check (✓) the words you know. Open your dictionary. Find the words you don't know.

> ### Word List: The Workplace
> **Dictionary pages 164–165**
>
> ☐ entrance ☐ safety regulations ☐ pay stub
>
> ☐ customer ☐ time clock ☐ wages
>
> ☐ office ☐ supervisor ☐ deductions
>
> ☐ employer/boss ☐ employee ☐ paycheque
>
> ☐ receptionist ☐ payroll clerk

2. Match the words with the pictures.

1.
I'm the boss.

2.
I answer the phones.

3.
I work here.

4.
I supervise the employees.

5.
I write the paycheques

_3_ **a.** employee   ___ **c.** payroll clerk   ___ **e.** employer

___ **b.** receptionist   ___ **d.** supervisor

3. Read the sentences. Circle the correct words.

a. Customers use the (entrance)/ time clock.

b. A receptionist works in the deductions / office.

c. The employees use the time clock / payroll.

d. The payroll clerk works with safety regulations / paycheques.

e. It's important for employees to have safety regulations / receptionists.

f. A pay stub shows the employee's boss / wages and deductions.

4. Label the picture. Write the numbers.

1. time clock

2. supervisor

3. employee entrance

4. safety regulations

5. ~~employee~~

5. Study the pay stub. Write _T_ (true) or _F_ (false).

Pay Period: 03072010

Employee Name: Ronald Jenkins

Employee Number: 24592

Earnings		Deductions			
Total Wages	$240.00			**Net Pay**	
		Federal	$12.50	(paycheque amount)	$211.51
		GPP	$ 1.44		
		EI	$14.55		

a. The employer's first name is Ronald. _F_

b. The payroll clerk's name is Net. ____

c. The employee's last name is Jenkins. ____

d. Ron's deductions are $240.00. ____

e. There are three kinds of deductions. ____

f. The total wages are $211.51. ____

Challenge Look at the deductions on the pay stub. What is the total?

1. Check (✓) the jobs you can do. Use your dictionary for help.

> ### Word List: Jobs and Occupations A–C
> Dictionary page 166
>
> ☐ accountant   ☐ babysitter   ☐ cashier
> ☐ assembler   ☐ business owner   ☐ childcare worker
> ☐ auto mechanic   ☐ businessperson

2. Complete the words. Write the letters.

a. b _a_ b y s _i_ t _t_ e r

b. b u __ i n e s __ p __ __ s __ n

c. __ s s e m __ l __ r

d. a __ __ o u n __ a n __

e. __ a s __ i __ __

3. Look at the pictures. Circle the correct words.

a. She's a cashier / (childcare worker.)

b. He's an auto mechanic / assembler.

c. She's a babysitter / businessperson.

d. He's a business owner / accountant.

e. He's an accountant / assembler.

f. She's a babysitter / cashier.

1. **Check (✓) the jobs that are interesting to you. Use your dictionary for help.**

> **Word List: Jobs and Occupations C–H**
> **Dictionary page 167**
>
> ☐ computer technician   ☐ firefighter   ☐ garment worker
>
> ☐ delivery person   ☐ florist   ☐ hairdresser
>
> ☐ dental assistant   ☐ gardener   ☐ home health care aide

2. **Match the words with the pictures.**

1.  2. 3.  4.  5.

_4_ **a.** firefighter   ___ **c.** computer technician   ___ **e.** garment worker

___ **b.** hairdresser   ___ **d.** delivery person

3. **Study the graph. Write the job names in order (1–5) starting with the highest salary.**

a. _____firefighter_____

b. _____

c. _____

d. _____

e. _____

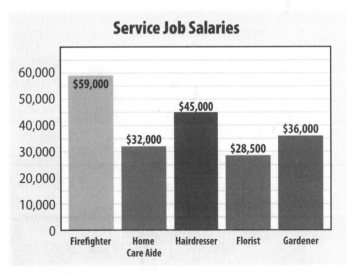

Service Job Salaries

Firefighter $59,000; Home Care Aide $32,000; Hairdresser $45,000; Florist $28,500; Gardener $36,000

Challenge Think about the jobs and the salaries in Exercise 3. Name the jobs you like. Write the jobs in order (1 = your favourite job).

Jobs and Occupations H–P

1. **Check (✓) three jobs people can do in a home. Use your dictionary for help.**

Word List: Jobs and Occupations H–P
Dictionary page 168

☐ homemaker   ☐ manicurist   ☐ musician

☐ housekeeper   ☐ messenger   ☐ nurse

☐ machine operator   ☐ mover   ☐ painter

2. **Unscramble the words.**

   a. hemokamer   h _o_ _m_ e _m_ a _k_ er

   b. runse   n ___ ___ ___ e

   c. iamcniruts   m ___ n i c ___ r ___ ___ t

   d. peintar   ___ a i ___ ___ ___ r

   e. engmesser   ___ e ___ ___ e n ___ ___ ___

   f. inmhace ratorpeo   m a ___ ___ i n ___   o p ___ r ___ t ___ r

3. **Label the picture. Use the words in the box.**

| painter | mover | housekeeper | musician | ~~nurse~~ |

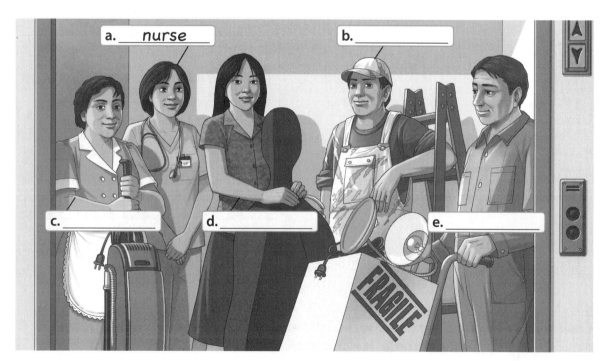

a. ___nurse___   b. _____

c. _____   d. _____   e. _____

1. Check (✓) the jobs you don't need a university degree for. Use your dictionary for help.

> ## Word List: Jobs and Occupations P–W
> ### Dictionary page 169
>
> ☐ postal worker   ☐ security guard   ☐ truck driver
>
> ☐ receptionist   ☐ social worker   ☐ veterinarian
>
> ☐ retail clerk   ☐ stock clerk   ☐ welder

2. Match the words with the sentences.

<u>5</u> **a.** postal worker

____ **b.** social worker

____ **c.** retail clerk

____ **d.** security guard

____ **e.** truck driver

____ **f.** welder

1. I help families and children.

2. I can fix machines, pipes, and cars.

3. I drive from Vancouver to Toronto every week.

4. I work in a clothing store.

5. I work at the post office.

6. I work in a bank.

3. Look at the pictures. Read the sentences. Number the people.

<u>4</u> **a.**    ____ **b.**    ____ **c.**

____ **d.**    ____ **e.**    ____ **f.**

1. Sam's a security guard.

2. Francisco's a retail clerk.

3. Maria's a veterinarian.

4. Kima's a postal worker.

5. Don's a truck driver.

6. Samir's a stock clerk.

Job Skills

1. **Check (✓) the things that are difficult to do. Use your dictionary for help.**

> ### Word List: Job Skills
> #### Dictionary page 170
>
> ☐ **do** manual labour   ☐ **repair** appliances   ☐ **supervise** people
>
> ☐ **drive** a truck   ☐ **sell** cars   ☐ **take care of** children
>
> ☐ **program** computers   ☐ **sew** clothes   ☐ **use** a cash register

2. **Match the words with the pictures.**

1.    2.    3.

4.    5.    6.

_2_ **a.** program computers   ___ **c.** repair appliances   ___ **e.** do manual labour

___ **b.** use a cash register   ___ **d.** supervise people   ___ **f.** sell cars

3. **Complete the sentences. Use the words in the box.**

> | | | |
> |---|---|---|
> | use a cash register | ~~drive a truck~~ | sew clothes |
> | take care of children | do manual labour | |

a. Deon is a truck driver. He can _drive a truck_____.

b. Karen is a childcare worker. She can _____.

c. Maya is a cashier. She can _____.

d. Adan is a garment worker. He can _____.

e. Dishi is a gardener. He can _____.

1. Check (✓) the things you can do. Use your dictionary for help.

> ### Word List: Office Skills
> Dictionary page 171
>
> ☐ **type** a letter   ☐ **staple**   ☐ **leave** a message
>
> ☐ **enter** data   ☐ **fax** a document   ☐ **take** a message
>
> ☐ **make** copies   ☐ **print** a document   ☐ **check** messages

2. Write the words in the chart. Use the words in the box.

> take a message   enter data   type a letter   leave a message
>
> make copies   ~~check messages~~   staple

	On the Phone	At the Copy Machine	At the Computer
a.	*check messages*	d.	f.
b.		e.	g.
c.			

3. Look at the pictures. Put the sentences in order (1–5).

___ He prints the letter.   ___ He puts the copies on his supervisor's desk.

___ He faxes the letter.   _1_ Hilal is typing a letter for his supervisor.

___ He makes copies of the letter.

Challenge Think about Hilal's office skills. Name four things he can do.

1. Check (✓) the words you know. Open your dictionary. Find the words you don't know.

> ### Word List: Career Planning
> #### Dictionary page 172
>
> **Career Path**
> - ☐ entry-level job
> - ☐ training
> - ☐ new job
> - ☐ promotion
>
> **Types of Job Training**
> - ☐ vocational training
> - ☐ internship
> - ☐ on-the-job training
>
> **Planning a Career**
> - ☐ career counsellor
> - ☐ job fair

2. Unscramble the sentences.

a. <u>It's an entry-level job.</u>

    an   It's   job.   entry-level

b. _____

    wants   Elda   promotion.   a

c. _____

    the   job   fair.   Come   to

d. _____

    a   career   counsellor.   He's

e. _____

    on-the-job   There's   training.

3. Read the ads. Check (✓) the correct ad.

1. **SALESPERSON WANTED**
Entry level. Train on the job.
Call Marty at
555-3692

2. **BROADCAST HELP**
Internship at TV station.
Promotion possible. Evenings
and weekends.
Apply at 254 South Street.

3. **JOBS! JOBS! JOBS!**
Center St. Job Fair Sunday 8-4.
• Visit 40 companies
• Talk to a career counselor
• Get information about
  vocational training

	Ad #1	Ad #2	Ad #3
a. There is on-the-job training at this job.	✓	☐	☐
b. This ad is for an internship.	☐	☐	☐
c. You can learn about vocational training here.	☐	☐	☐
d. You can get a promotion at this job.	☐	☐	☐
e. This is a beginning level job.	☐	☐	☐
f. There are jobs, counsellors, and information here.	☐	☐	☐

  **See page 301 for listening practice.**

1. **Check (✓) the ways to find a job. Use your dictionary for help.**

> **Word List: Job Search**
> **Dictionary page 173**
>
> ☐ **talk** to friends   ☐ **write** a resume
>
> ☐ **look in** the classifieds   ☐ **fill out** an application
>
> ☐ **look for** help wanted signs   ☐ **go on** an interview
>
> ☐ **check** Internet job sites   ☐ **get** hired

2. **Match the words.**

   _1_ **a.** get   **1.** hired

   ___ **b.** talk to   **2.** classifieds

   ___ **c.** write a   **3.** interview

   ___ **d.** fill out an   **4.** friends

   ___ **e.** go on an   **5.** resume

   ___ **f.** look in the   **6.** application

3. **Study the chart. Complete the sentences. Use the words in the box.**

> classifieds   talk   Internet   help wanted   ~~check~~

   a. Forty percent ___*check*___ Internet job sites.

   b. Thirty percent _____ to friends and family.

   c. Fifteen percent look for _____ signs.

   d. Fifteen percent look in the _____.

   e. Sixty percent don't check _____ job sites.

How Students at Cartier Adult School Look for Jobs

40%   30%   15%   15%

■ friends and family
■ classifieds
■ help wanted signs
■ Internet

Interview Skills

1. Check (✓) the things to do before an interview. Use your dictionary for help.

> ## Word List: Interview Skills
> ### Dictionary page 174
>
> ☐ **Prepare** for the interview ☐ **Don't** be late ☐ **Listen** carefully
> ☐ **Be** neat ☐ **Turn off** your cellphone ☐ **Ask** questions
> ☐ **Bring** your resume and ID ☐ **Shake** hands ☐ **Write** a thank-you note

2. Match the words with the pictures.

1.  2.  3.

4.  5.

__4__ **a.** Turn off your cellphone.   ___ **c.** Write a thank-you note.   ___ **e.** Don't be late.

___ **b.** Shake hands.   ___ **d.** Bring your ID.

3. Complete the crossword puzzle.

Across

1. ___ for the interview.

3. ___ carefully.

5. ___ questions.

Down

2. Bring your ___.

3. Don't be ___.

4. Be ___.

(Crossword: 1 Across = PREPARE)

1. **Check (✓) the words you know. Open your dictionary. Find the words you don't know.**

> **Word List: A Factory**
> **Dictionary page 175**
>
> ☐ factory owner   ☐ assembly line   ☐ forklift
> ☐ factory worker   ☐ warehouse   ☐ shipping clerk
> ☐ parts   ☐ conveyor belt   ☐ loading dock

2. **Complete the chart. Use all the words in the Word List.**

Places at Work	Things at Work	People at Work
a. *assembly line*	d.	g.
b.	e.	h.
c.	f.	i.

3. **Label the picture. Use the words in the box.**

> factory worker   factory owner   assembly line   conveyor belt   parts   ~~factory~~

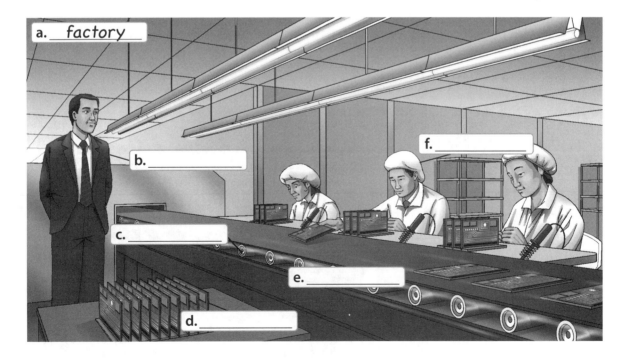

a. *factory*
b. _____
c. _____
d. _____
e. _____
f. _____

Challenge Name three things from the Word List that are NOT in the picture.

1. Check (✓) the words you know. Open your dictionary. Find the words you don't know.

> ### Word List: Landscaping and Gardening
> #### Dictionary page 176
>
> | | | |
> |---|---|---|
> | ☐ leaf blower | ☐ rake | ☐ **trim** the hedges |
> | ☐ lawn mower | ☐ hedge clippers | ☐ **rake** the leaves |
> | ☐ shovel | ☐ **mow** the lawn | ☐ **plant** a tree |

2. Match the words with the pictures.

1.

2.

3.

4.

5.

__5__ **a.** leaf blower   ____ **c.** lawn mower   ____ **e.** hedge clippers

____ **b.** rake   ____ **d.** shovel

3. Look at the pictures. Complete the sentences.

a. Tim will mow the lawn for ___$12.00___ .

b. Tim will plant a tree for _____ .

c Tim will trim the hedges for _____ .

d. Tim will rake the leaves and plant a tree for _____ .

e. Tim will mow the lawn, trim the hedges, and rake the leaves for _____ .

Farming and Ranching

1. **Check (✓) the things that grow on a farm. Use your dictionary for help.**

Word List: Farming and Ranching
Dictionary page 177

☐ rice   ☐ field   ☐ hay

☐ wheat   ☐ barn   ☐ rancher

☐ soybeans   ☐ farmer

☐ corn   ☐ livestock

2. **Write the words in the chart. Use the words in the box.**

| rice | farmer | ~~field~~ | barn | rancher | soybeans | wheat |

	Places		People		Plants
a.	field	c.		e.	
b.		d.		f.	
				g.	

3. **Look at the picture. Write _T_ (true) or _F_ (false).**

a. The farmer is in the barn.   _T_

b. The farmer has livestock. _____

c. The farmer is putting corn on the truck. _____

e. The truck is in the field. _____

d. The hay is in the truck. _____

f. There are soybeans on the truck. _____

177

🔧 Construction

1. Check (✓) the words you know. Open your dictionary. Find the words you don't know.

> ## Word List: Construction
> ### Dictionary page 178
>
> | | | |
> |---|---|---|
> | ☐ construction worker | ☐ tile | ☐ **paint** |
> | ☐ ladder | ☐ bricks | ☐ **lay** bricks |
> | ☐ concrete | ☐ wood | ☐ **install** tile |

2. Complete the words. Write the letters.

a. w _o_ _o_ d

b. l a ___ ___ e ___

c. t ___ ___ e

d. b ___ ___ c ___ s

e. ___ o n c ___ ___ ___ e

f. c o ___ s t ___ ___ c ___ i o ___   w ___ ___ ___ e r

3. Look at the picture. Read the sentences. Number the people.

a. _5_   b. ____   c. ____   d. ____   e. ____   f. ____

1. Mario is installing tile.
2. Ben has a ladder.
3. Tisha is painting.
4. Ali is laying bricks.
5. Max is working with concrete.
6. Luis is getting more bricks.

1. Check (✓) the things that are not safe. Use your dictionary for help.

> **Word List: Job Safety**
> **Dictionary page 179**
>
> ☐ careless worker   ☐ slippery floor   ☐ knee pads
> ☐ careful worker   ☐ safety goggles   ☐ safety boots
> ☐ broken equipment   ☐ ear plugs   ☐ fire extinguisher

2. Match the words with the sentences.

_5_ **a.** broken equipment   **1.** It protects you from fire.

___ **b.** fire extinguisher   **2.** They protect your knees.

___ **c.** slippery floor   **3.** They protect your eyes.

___ **d.** safety goggles   **4.** They protect your feet.

___ **e.** safety boots   **5.** It's not safe to use this at work.

___ **f.** knee pads   **6.** It's not safe to walk here.

3. Look at the pictures. Check (✓) the correct sentences.

a. ☑ He's using his ear plugs.
   ☐ He's using broken equipment.

b. ☐ She's wearing safety boots.
   ☐ She's wearing knee pads.

c. ☐ He's careless.
   ☐ The floor is slippery.

d. ☐ The extinguisher is broken.
   ☐ He's a careful worker.

1. **Check (✓) the things you have at home. Use your dictionary for help.**

> ### Word List: Tools and Building Supplies
> #### Dictionary pages 180–181
>
> | | | |
> |---|---|---|
> | ☐ hammer | ☐ 2 x 4 (two by four) | ☐ screw |
> | ☐ handsaw | ☐ paintbrush | ☐ nail |
> | ☐ electric drill | ☐ paint roller | ☐ tape measure |
> | ☐ extension cord | ☐ paint | ☐ duct tape |
> | ☐ pipe | ☐ screwdriver | ☐ sandpaper |

2. **Cross out the word that doesn't belong.**

   a. ~~paint roller~~   extension cord   electric drill

   b. paint   duct tape   paintbrush

   c. sandpaper   screw   nail

   d. screwdriver   screw   2 x 4

   e. hammer   pipe   nail

3. **Read the labels. Draw the pictures.**

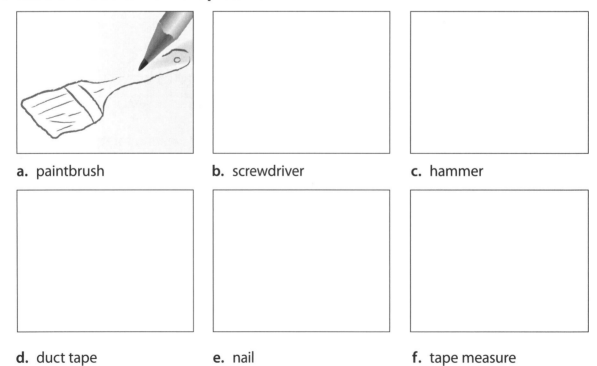

   a. paintbrush   b. screwdriver   c. hammer

   d. duct tape   e. nail   f. tape measure

4. Answer the questions. Use the words in the box.

a handsaw	a nail	a hammer	a paintbrush	~~a tape measure~~
2 x 4s	paint	a drill	a paint roller	screws

a. What does John need?

   a tape measure

   _____

   _____

b. What does Irene need?

   _____

   _____

   _____

c. What does Ron need?

   _____

   _____

   _____

   _____

5. What about you? Answer the questions.

a. What tools and supplies do you usually use? _____

b. Where do you buy tools and supplies? _____

c. Where do you keep your tools and supplies? _____

Challenge Name three tools and supplies that are expensive. Name three that are cheap. Make a list.

1. **Check (✓) the words you know. Open your dictionary. Find the words you don't know.**

> **Word List: An Office**
> Dictionary page 182
>
> ☐ supply cabinet   ☐ office manager   ☐ computer technician
> ☐ conference room   ☐ file clerk   ☐ reception area
> ☐ cubicle   ☐ file cabinet

2. **Complete the chart. Use all the words in the Word List.**

People	Places	Things
a. *office manager*	d.	g.
b.	e.	h.
c.	f.	

3. **Complete the sentences. Circle the correct words.**

a. Maria is in the <u>conference room</u> / <u>(reception area)</u>.

b. She's a <u>file clerk / receptionist</u>.

c. Zahra is the <u>office manager / receptionist</u>.

d. She's in the <u>file / conference room</u>.

e. Victor is a <u>computer technician / file clerk</u>.

f. He's putting files in the <u>reception area / file cabinet</u>.

g. Linda is <u>an office manager / a computer technician</u>.

h. She's fixing a computer in a <u>cubicle / conference room</u>.

4. Check (✓) the things you use at home or at work. Use your dictionary for help.

> ### Word List: An Office
> Dictionary page 183
>
> **Office Equipment**
> ☐ computer
> ☐ printer
> ☐ scanner
> ☐ fax machine
> ☐ photocopier
>
> **Office Supplies**
> ☐ stapler
> ☐ staples
> ☐ paper clip
> ☐ glue

5. Unscramble the words.

a. spatles   s _t_ a _p_ _l_ e _s_

b. leug   g __ u __

c. rentpri   p __ i __ t e __

d. nerscan   s __ __ n n __ __

e. cupemtor   __ o m __ u __ e __

f. eppar plic   __ __ p e __   __ l i __

6. Label the picture. Use the words in the box.

| computer | fax machine | glue | paper clips | stapler | printer | ~~photocopier~~ |

a. *photocopier*
b. _____
c. _____
d. _____
e. _____
f. _____
g. _____

See page 304 for listening practice.

A Hotel

1. **Check (✓) the hotel jobs. Use your dictionary for help.**

Word List: A Hotel

Dictionary page 184

- ☐ doorman
- ☐ parking attendant
- ☐ bellhop

- ☐ luggage cart
- ☐ desk clerk
- ☐ front desk

- ☐ guest room
- ☐ room service
- ☐ housekeeper

2. **Match the words.**

_5_ **a.** guest   **1.** cart

___ **b.** luggage   **2.** clerk

___ **c.** room   **3.** attendant

___ **d.** front   **4.** desk

___ **e.** desk   **5.** room

___ **f.** parking   **6.** service

3. **Look at the picture. Read the sentences. Number the people.**

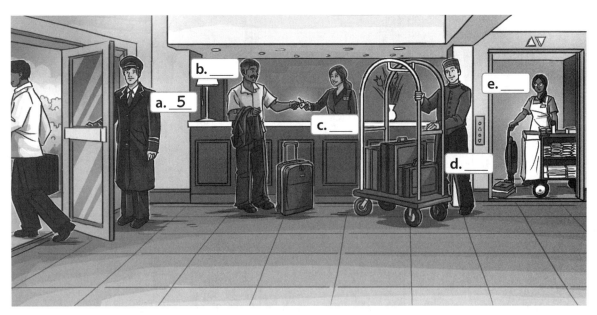

1. Leela is a housekeeper.
2. Elena is a desk clerk.
3. Amal is a guest at the hotel.
4. Ken is a bellhop.
5. Ron is a doorman.

1. Check (✓) the food service jobs. Use your dictionary for help.

Word List: Food Service
Dictionary page 185

☐ short-order cook   ☐ storeroom   ☐ diner

☐ dishwasher   ☐ head chef   ☐ buffet

☐ walk-in freezer   ☐ server   ☐ head waiter

---

2. Unscramble the sentences.

a. in The dishwasher the is kitchen.   _The dishwasher is in the kitchen._

b. servers food. the bring The   _____

c. at The diners the buffet. are   _____

d. There's in meat walk-in freezer. the   _____

e. in The storeroom. head chef is the   _____

3. What's wrong with the picture? Circle the correct words.

a. The (diner) / head chef is washing dishes.

b. The diner / dishwasher is eating.

c. The head chef is sleeping in the storeroom / freezer.

d. The storeroom / kitchen doesn't have any food.

e. The cook / head waiter is eating the soup.

f. The walk-in freezer / buffet is open.

A Bad Day at Work

1. Check (✓) the words you know. Open your dictionary. Find the words you don't know.

Word List: A Bad Day at Work
Dictionary pages 186–187

☐ dangerous	☐ floor plan	☐ wiring
☐ clinic	☐ contractor	☐ bricklayer
☐ budget	☐ electrical hazard	☐ **call in** sick

2. Match the words with the pictures.

1.

2.
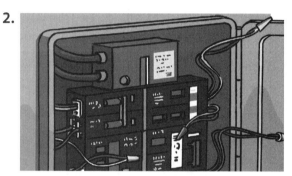

3.

4.
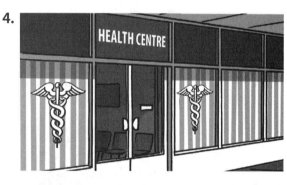

5.

6.

__5__ **a.** contractor   ___ **c.** clinic   ___ **e.** wiring

___ **b.** bricklayer   ___ **d.** electrical hazard   ___ **f.** floor plan

4. Look at the pictures. Circle the correct words.

a. Sam is a good customer / (contractor.)

b. He and the customer are looking at the
floor plan / bricklayer.

c. Next they will look at the budget / bricklayer.

d. Construction work can be careful / dangerous.

e. Sam always looks for electrical hazards
and bad budgets / wiring.

f. Sam is having a bad day / hazard today.
He hurt his back.

g. He's dangerous / at the clinic.

h. The doctor says he can't wire / work all week.

i. Poor Sam. He doesn't like to be a contractor /
call in sick.

5. What about you? Answer the questions.

a. Do you have a dangerous job? _____

b. Do you know other people with dangerous jobs? _____

c. Name three jobs you think are dangerous.

Use your dictionary for help. _____ _____ _____

1. **Check (✓) the words you know. Open your dictionary. Find the words you don't know.**

Word List: Schools and Subjects
Dictionary page 188

☐ preschool   ☐ high school   ☐ university

☐ elementary school   ☐ vocational school   ☐ adult school

☐ middle school   ☐ college

2. **Label the schools. Use the words in the box.**

preschool   elementary school   ~~high school~~   vocational school   adult school

a. _____high school_____   b. _____   c. _____

d. _____   e. _____

3. **Read the sentences. Circle the correct words.**

a. Tina is seven years old. She goes to preschool / (elementary school.)

b. Brandon is three. He goes to preschool / vocational school.

c. Mike studies electronics. He goes to vocational /middle school.

d. Sun is 16 years old. She goes to middle / high school.

e. Omar is in medical school. He goes to a college / university.

f. Minh learns English at the community centre. She goes to middle / adult school.

4. Check (✓) the things you like to study. Use your dictionary for help.

Word List: Schools and Subjects
Dictionary page 189

- ☐ language arts
- ☐ history
- ☐ arts
- ☐ math
- ☐ world languages
- ☐ music
- ☐ science
- ☐ ESL
- ☐ physical education

5. Match the words with the pictures.

<u>3</u> **a.** music

___ **b.** science

___ **c.** ESL

___ **d.** math

___ **e.** history

___ **f.** world languages

1.
2.
3.
4.
5.
6.

6. Study the chart. Complete the sentences.

a. Forty percent of students like <u>Language Arts</u>.

b. Ten percent of students like _____.

c. Forty-five percent of students like math and _____.

d. Five percent of students like _____.

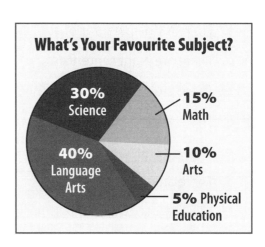

What's Your Favourite Subject?

30% Science
15% Math
40% Language Arts
10% Arts
5% Physical Education

Challenge What's your favourite subject? Ask three people. Write their answers.

English Composition

1. Check (✓) the words you know. Open your dictionary. Find the words you don't know.

Word List: English Composition
Dictionary page 190

- ☐ word
- ☐ sentence
- ☐ paragraph
- ☐ period
- ☐ question mark
- ☐ exclamation mark
- ☐ comma
- ☐ quotation marks
- ☐ apostrophe

2. Follow the directions.

a. Circle the period.
There's my book.

b. Circle the quotation marks.
"Be careful!"

c. Circle the word with an apostrophe.
Where is Tom's car?

d. Circle the question mark.
What's on your desk?

e. Circle the commas.
There's a desk, a chair, and a pencil.

f. Circle the exclamation mark.
The police officer said, "Stop!"

3. Read the paragraph. Circle the punctuation. Then write *T* (true) or *F* (false).

Today we are studying English composition. We're learning about sentences and punctuation. I know that sentences need a period, a question mark, or an exclamation mark. Some words need apostrophes. Do you know how to use quotation marks?

a. There is one paragraph.   _T_

b. There are eight sentences.   ____

c. There are two commas.   ____

d. There are two question marks.   ____

e. There is one apostrophe.   ____

f. There are 25 words.   ____

4. Check (✓) the things you like to do. Use your dictionary for help.

> ### Word List: English Composition
> #### Dictionary page 191
>
> ☐ **Brainstorm** ideas ☐ **Write** a first draft ☐ **Rewrite**
> ☐ **Organize** your ideas ☐ **Edit** ☐ **Turn in** your paper

5. Match the words with the pictures.

1.
2.
3.

4.
5.
6.

_1_ **a.** write   ___ **c.** turn in   ___ **e.** edit

___ **b.** brainstorm   ___ **d.** organize   ___ **f.** rewrite

6. Complete the sentences. Use the words in the box.

> ideas   organize   ~~composition~~   draft   rewrite   turn in

a. The students are writing a _composition_ .

b. They brainstorm _____.

c. They _____ their ideas.

d. They write a first _____.

e. They edit and _____ their work.

f. Then they _____ their papers.

Mathematics

1. **Check (✓) the words you know. Open your dictionary. Find the words you don't know.**

   > ### Word List: Mathematics
   > **Dictionary page 192**
   >
   > ☐ negative integers ☐ add
   > ☐ positive integers ☐ subtract
   > ☐ odd numbers ☐ multiply
   > ☐ even numbers ☐ divide

2. **Match the numbers with the words.**

   <u>4</u> **a.** 1, 3, 5   1. positive three

   ___ **b.** −3   2. even number

   ___ **c.** 2   3. negative three

   ___ **d.** 3   4. odd numbers

   ___ **e.** 10 + 2   5. add

   ___ **f.** 10 × 2   6. subtract

   ___ **g.** 10 ÷ 2   7. multiply

   ___ **h.** 10 − 2   8. divide

3. **Do the math. Then circle all the correct letters.**

   a. $4 \times 4 =$ <u>16</u>

   b. $2 - 6 =$ ___

   c. $7 + 2 =$ ___

   d. $9 \div 3 =$ ___

   1. This problem has a negative answer.   a   (b)   c   d
   2. This problem has no even numbers.   a   b   c   d
   3. These problems have no odd numbers.   a   b   c   d
   4. These problems have positive answers.   a   b   c   d

4. **Check (✓) the lines, shapes, and angles you see in your classroom. Use your dictionary for help.**

> **Word List: Mathematics**
> **Dictionary page 193**
>
> ☐ straight line   ☐ right angle   ☐ triangle
> ☐ curved line   ☐ rectangle   ☐ circle
> ☐ parallel lines   ☐ square

5. **Cross out the word that doesn't belong.**

   a. straight   ~~right~~   curved

   b. rectangle   square   circle

   c. triangle   square   curved line

   d. triangle   circle   curved line

   e. right angle   parallel lines   straight line

6. **Read the labels. Draw the pictures.**

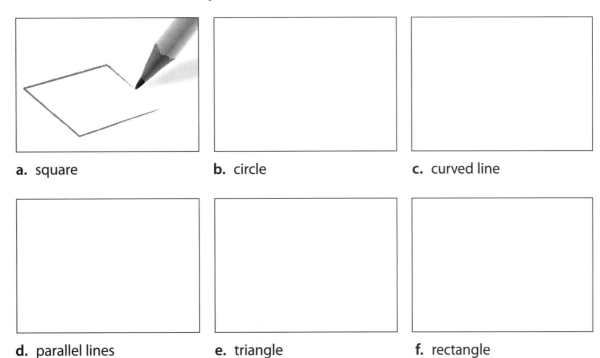

   a. square   **b.** circle   **c.** curved line

   d. parallel lines **e.** triangle   **f.** rectangle

Challenge How many lines are in a square? A triangle? A circle?

1. **Check (✓) the things a biologist can see with a microscope. Use your dictionary for help.**

> ### Word List: Science
> #### Dictionary page 194
>
> **Biology**
> ☐ organisms   ☐ slide
> ☐ biologist   ☐ cell
>   ☐ nucleus
>
> **Microscope**
> ☐ eyepiece   ☐ base
> ☐ stage   ☐ arm

2. **Read the sentences. Circle the correct words.**

   a. A biologist studies (biology) / a base.

   b. All organisms have slides / cells.

   c. Every cell has a nucleus / an arm.

   d. A biologist uses a microscope / nucleus to see small organisms.

   e. Put the slide on the eyepiece / stage.

   f. Use the base / eyepiece to see the slide.

3. **Label the pictures. Use the words in the box.**

   | stage | ~~eyepiece~~ | slide | base | arm |

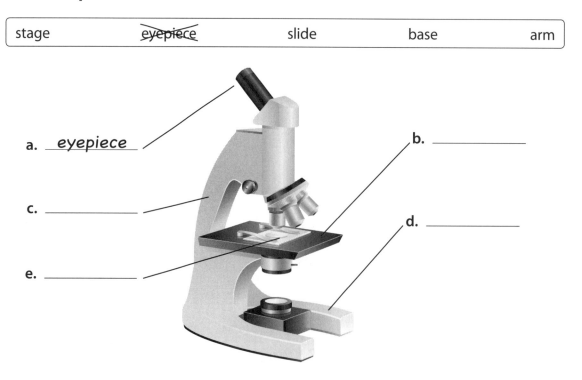

   a. _eyepiece_

   b. _____

   c. _____

   d. _____

   e. _____

4. Check (✓) the things a chemist studies. Use your dictionary for help.

Word List: Science
Dictionary page 195

Chemistry		A Science Lab	
☐ chemist	☐ molecule	☐ Bunsen burner	☐ forceps
☐ periodic table	☐ atom	☐ beaker	☐ dropper
		☐ test tube	

5. Unscramble the words.

a. karbee b _e_ _a_ k _e_ _r_

b. sitmhec c __ __ m __ __ t

c. preorpd d __ __ p p __ __

d. mtao __ __ __ m

e. focresp __ o r __ __ p __

f. clueelom m __ l __ c __ __ __

6. Look at the picture. Circle the correct words.

a. There are three (test tubes)/ beakers.

b. The <u>chemist / periodic table</u> is working.

c. The <u>droppers / forceps</u> are next to the Bunsen burner.

d. There are four <u>test tubes / droppers</u>.

e. The chemist is studying <u>molecules / a Bunsen burner</u>.

1. Check (✓) the things you use or do every day. Use your dictionary for help.

Word List: Computers
Dictionary page 196

☐ hard drive	☐ keyboard	☐ **type**
☐ DVD and CD-ROM drive	☐ mouse	☐ **select**
☐ software	☐ printer	☐ **delete**
☐ monitor		

2. Match the words with the sentences.

_5_ **a.** hard drive

____ **b.** mouse

____ **c.** keyboard

____ **d.** DVD and CD-ROM drive

____ **e.** printer

1. Use this to type.

2. Put a CD-ROM here.

3. Use this to select words.

4. Use this to print documents.

5. The computer keeps information here.

3. Label the picture. Use the words in the box.

printer	software	monitor	keyboard	mouse	~~CD-ROM drive~~

a. CD-ROM drive

b. _____

c. _____

d. _____

e. _____

f. _____

1. **Check (✓) the words you know. Open your dictionary. Find the words you don't know.**

> **Word List: The Internet**
> **Dictionary page 197**
>
> ☐ menu bar   ☐ pointer   ☐ **address** the email
> ☐ back button   ☐ cursor   ☐ **type** the message
> ☐ URL / website address ☐ scroll bar   ☐ **send** the email

2. **Unscramble the words.**

    a. emun rba   m _e_ _n_ u b _a_ r

    b. ruoscr   c __ __ s __ r

    c. trepion   p __ i __ t __ __

    d. stiebwe   w __ __ s __ __ e

    e. orcsll abr   s __ __ o __ l b __ __

    f. kabc notbut   b __ __ k
                          b __ __ __ __ n

3. **Label the pictures. Write the numbers.**

    _4_ **a.**    __ **b.**    __ **c.**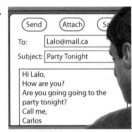

    __ **d.**    __ **e.**    __ **f.**

    1. Read the email.   **3.** Select the word.   **5.** Delete the mistake.

    2. Send the email.   **4.** Address the email.   **6.** Type the message.

1. **Check (✓) the wars you know about. Use your dictionary for help.**

Word List: Canadian History
Dictionary page 198

☐ provinces   ☐ British North America Act   ☐ War of 1812

☐ settlers   ☐ Battle of the Plains of Abraham   ☐ World War I

☐ First Nations   ☐ Fathers of Confederation   ☐ World War II

☐ Great Depression

2. **Take the test. Fill in the answers.**

Name: _____   Date: _____

1. Ⓐ ● Ⓒ Ⓓ   3. Ⓐ Ⓑ Ⓒ Ⓓ   5. Ⓐ Ⓑ Ⓒ Ⓓ

2. Ⓐ Ⓑ Ⓒ Ⓓ   4. Ⓐ Ⓑ Ⓒ Ⓓ   6. Ⓐ Ⓑ Ⓒ Ⓓ

1. Name the conflict between the British and the French.
   a. War of 1812
   b. Battle of the Plains of Abraham

2. Name the war in which the U.S. fought the British and Canada.
   a. World War II
   b. War of 1812

3. Who created the British North America Act?
   a. the settlers
   b. the Fathers of Confederation

4. Name the first people to live in North America.
   a. First Nations people
   b. settlers

5. Name the first people from Europe to live in North America.
   a. Inuit
   b. settlers

6. Name the World War from 1939–1945.
   a. World War I
   b. World War II

Challenge If you were moving to a new country, what would you take with you and why?

 See page 306 for listening practice.

1. **Check (✓) the words you know. Open your dictionary. Find the words you don't know.**

> **Word List: World History**
> **Dictionary page 199**
>
> ☐ exploration   ☐ army   ☐ invention
> ☐ explorer   ☐ immigration   ☐ inventor
> ☐ war   ☐ immigrant

2. **Complete the words. Write the letters.**

a. e _x_ p l _o_ r e _r_

b. a ___ ___ y

c. ___ ___ r

d. ___ n v ___ n t ___ ___ n

e. ___ m m ___ g ___ a ___ ___

f. e x ___ ___ o ___ a t ___ ___ ___

3. **Look at the pictures. Circle the correct words.**

a. Alexander Graham Bell was an (inventor)/ explorer.

b. The telephone was an important invention / composition.

c. Albert Einstein was a famous dictator / immigrant. He left Europe in 1933.

d. Marco Polo was an explorer/ composer. He went to China.

North America and Central America

1. **Check (✓) the places you know. Open your dictionary. Find the places you don't know.**

> ### Word List: North America and Central America
> #### Dictionary pages 200–201
>
> ☐ Atlantic Ocean ☐ Canada ☐ Guatemala ☐ Nicaragua
>
> ☐ Pacific Ocean ☐ the United States of America ☐ Belize ☐ Costa Rica
>
> ☐ Gulf of Mexico ☐ Mexico ☐ El Salvador ☐ Panama
>
> ☐ Honduras

2. **Write the words in the chart. Use the words in the box.**

> Mexico   Panama   ~~Atlantic Ocean~~   Gulf of Mexico   Canada   Guatemala

Water	North America	Central America
a. Atlantic Ocean	c.	e.
b.	d.	f.

3. **Label the map. Write the numbers.**

1. Atlantic Ocean

2. ~~Pacific Ocean~~

3. Gulf of Mexico

4. Canada

5. the United States of America

6. Mexico

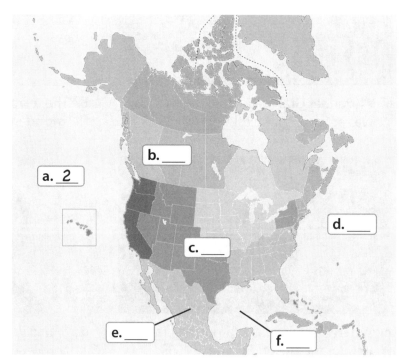

a. 2   b. ___   c. ___   d. ___   e. ___   f. ___

4. Look at the pictures. Write *T* (true) or *F* (false).

a. There are seven countries in Central America.   *T*

b. Belize is next to Mexico.   _____

c. Panama is next to Honduras.   _____

d. Mexico is in Central America.   _____

e. Mexico is between the Atlantic Ocean and the Gulf of Mexico.   _____

f. Mexico is next to Costa Rica and Nicaragua.   _____

g. The United States is between the Atlantic Ocean and the Pacific Ocean.   _____

h. The Atlantic Ocean is between the United States and Canada.   _____

i. Mexico is in Canada.   _____

5. Study the chart. Write the countries in order, from largest to smallest.

a. _United States_

b. _____

c. _____

d. _____

e. _____

Country	Number of People
Canada	33,487,000
El Salvador	7,185,000
Guatemala	13,277,000
Mexico	111,212,000
United States	307,212,000

See page 307 for listening practice.

1. Where is your country? Check (✓) the continent. Use your dictionary for help.

> **Word List: World Map**
> Dictionary pages 202–203
>
> | Continents | | Directions |
> |---|---|---|
> | ☐ North America | ☐ Africa | ☐ North |
> | ☐ South America | ☐ Australia | ☐ South |
> | ☐ Europe | ☐ Antarctica | ☐ East |
> | ☐ Asia | | ☐ West |

2. Unscramble the words.

a. rouEpe _____Europe_____   d. ustlAraia _____

b. caifrA _____   e. thouS mercaiA _____

c. saAi _____   f. orNth caimAer _____

d. tartcAnica _____   h. orlwd mpa _____

3. Label the compass. Use the words in the box.

> ~~North~~   South   East   West

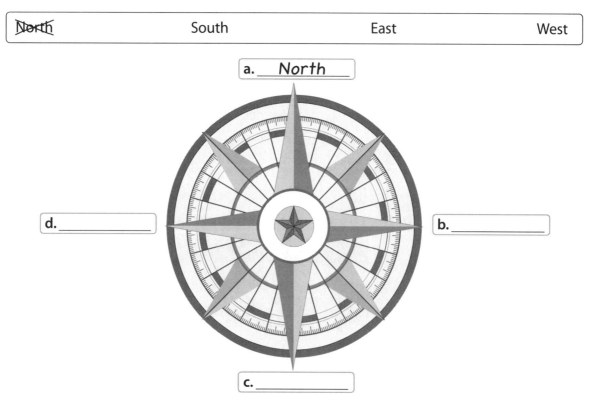

a. ___North___

d. _____

b. _____

c. _____

4. Look at the map. Circle the correct words.

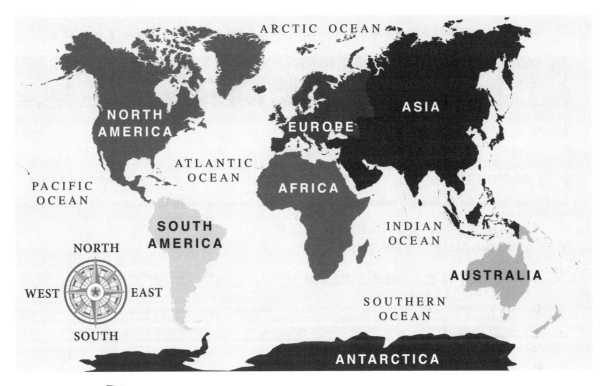

a. There are (seven) / nine continents.

b. There are three / five oceans.

c. Africa is south / east of Europe.

d. The Indian Ocean is between Africa, Asia, and South America / Australia.

e. Asia is east / north of Europe.

f. The Atlantic / Pacific Ocean is east of North and South America.

5. Study the chart. Put the continents in order, from largest to smallest.

a. _____Asia_____

b. _____

c. _____

d. _____

e. _____

f. _____

g. _____

Continent	Size (square miles)
Africa	39,065,000
Antarctica	13,209,000
Asia	44,579,000
Australia	7,687,000
Europe	9,938,000
North America	24,256,000
South America	17,819,000

Challenge Which continent has the most people? Which continent has the most countries?

Geography and Habitats

1. **Check (✓) the places in your home country. Use your dictionary for help.**

Word List: Geography and Habitats
Dictionary page 204

☐ rainforest   ☐ ocean   ☐ forest

☐ river   ☐ island   ☐ lake

☐ desert   ☐ beach   ☐ mountain range

---

2. **Match to complete the sentences.**

<u>5</u> **a.** Winnipeg is the name of a city and a   **1.** desert.

___ **b.** The Pacific is an   **2.** ocean.

___ **c.** Hawaii is a group of   **3.** river.

___ **d.** The Andes is a   **4.** islands.

___ **e.** The Sahara is a   **5.** lake.

___ **f.** The Nile is a   **6.** mountain range.

3. **Look at the pictures. Circle the correct words.**

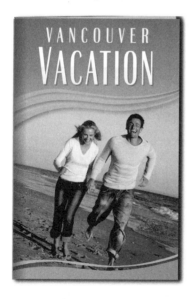

a. Do you like the <u>forest /</u>(<u>ocean</u>)? Come to the Vancouver <u>river / beaches</u>.

b. Do you need to relax? How about a quiet <u>ocean / lake</u> in the <u>forest / desert</u>?

c. Are you looking for an exciting place? Come to South America. See the <u>rainforest / desert</u>. Take a trip on the <u>river / mountain range</u>.

1. **Check (✓) the words you know. Open your dictionary. Find the words you don't know.**

> **Word List: The Universe**
> Dictionary page 205
>
> **Planets**
>
> ☐ Mercury ☐ Jupiter ☐ moon (new, full)
>
> ☐ Venus ☐ Saturn ☐ star
>
> ☐ Earth ☐ Uranus ☐ galaxy
>
> ☐ Mars ☐ Neptune

2. **Cross out the word that doesn't belong.**

    a. Mars ~~star~~ Earth

    b. Jupiter full moon new moon

    c. Earth Mercury galaxy

    d. star Mars moon

    e. planets stars universe

3. **Complete the crossword puzzle.**

    ACROSS

    2. Earth, Mars, and Venus are ___.

    5. a full or new ___

    6. the planet we live on

    DOWN

    1. a large group of stars

    3. a cold planet far from the sun

    4. The sun is a ___.

2 P L A N E T S

1. **Check (✓) the words you know. Open your dictionary. Find the words you don't know.**

☐ photographer	☐ podium	☐ **take** a picture
☐ funny photo	☐ ceremony	☐ **cry**
☐ serious photo	☐ cap	☐ **celebrate**
☐ guest speaker	☐ gown	

2. **Match the words with the pictures.**

_3_ **a.** guest speaker

___ **b.** gown

___ **c.** podium

___ **d.** photographer

___ **e.** cap

___ **f.** serious photo

___ **g.** funny photo

___ **h.** cry

1.

2.

3.
Thank you.

4.

5.

6.

7.

8.

3. **Read the story. Circle the correct words.**

   a. Here are some photos of my son's
      graduation (ceremony) / photographer.

   b. There's Ahmed in his cap and
      podium / gown.

   c. It's a very serious / funny photo.

   d. This is the guest speaker /photograph.

   e. He's in a cap / at the podium.

   f. This is Ahmed's favourite
      ceremony / photo.

   g. Ahmed is crying / celebrating with
      his friends.

   h. It's a very funny / serious photo.

4. **What about you? Answer the questions. Write _Yes, I do_ or _No, I don't_.**

   a. Do you like to take pictures? _____.

   b. Do you like people to take your picture? _____.

   c. Do you like to look at photos of other people? _____.

1. **Check (✓) the words you know. Open your dictionary.
    Find the words you don't know.**

> ## Word List: Nature Centre
> ### Dictionary pages 208–209
>
> ☐ trees ☐ plants ☐ sky ☐ nest
> ☐ soil ☐ rock ☐ mammals ☐ water
> ☐ path ☐ flowers ☐ insects ☐ fish
> ☐ bird ☐ sun

2. **Cross out the word that doesn't belong.**

    a. ~~flower~~   bird   nest

    b. sun   sky   soil

    c. tree   mammal   plant

    d. fish   insect   sun

    e. water   rocks   path

3. **Look at the picture. Read the sentences. Number the people.**

1. Mai is watching the birds.
2. Alma is looking at the flowers.
3. Mel is walking on the path.
4. Sam sees a fish.
5. Tony is sitting under the tree.
6. Hyun Jin is sitting on the rock.

4. Complete the story. Use the words in the box.

| insects | ~~nature~~ | nest | sky | centre | sun | birds |

a. Tina and Tim are at the ___nature___ centre today.

b. The _____ is warm.

c. The _____ is clear. It's a great day.

d. Tim is studying _____ for his science class.

e. Tina is watching the _____.

f. They have baby birds in their _____.

g. The nature _____ is a great place to learn.

5. Read the brochure. Answer the questions.

Bug Out! Learn all about insects.

Bird is the Word
Come see our bird show with 10 different birds.
Saturday 10-11

Lions, Tigers, and Bears
Come and watch them eat lunch.
Sunday 12-1

Take a picture with Isaac The Insect.
Wednesday 6-7

a. What can you learn about at Bug Out!? _____

b. How many birds can you see at the bird show? _____

c. When can you learn about mammals? _____

Trees and Plants

1. **Check (✓) the trees and plants in your neighbourhood. Use your dictionary for help.**

> **Word List: Trees and Plants**
> **Dictionary page 210**
>
> ☐ branch   ☐ pine   ☐ cactus
> ☐ trunk   ☐ palm   ☐ vine
> ☐ root   ☐ oak   ☐ poison ivy
> ☐ leaf

2. **Label the trees and plants. Use the words in the box.**

> ~~cactus~~   vine   palm tree   poison ivy   pine tree   oak tree

a. _____cactus_____   b. _____   c. _____

d. _____   e. _____   f. _____

3. **Read the sentences. Write _T_ (true) or _F_ (false).**

a. The leaves grow on the trunk of a tree.   _F_

b. The roots are on the branches.   ____

c. Branches grow from the trunk of a tree.   ____

d. Leaves grow on the branches.   ____

e. All trees have roots.   ____

f. All plants have trunks.   ____

1. Check (✓) the parts of a flower above the soil. Use your dictionary for help.

> **Word List: Flowers**
> **Dictionary page 211**
>
> ☐ seed   ☐ bud   ☐ sunflower
> ☐ roots   ☐ petals   ☐ tulip
> ☐ leaves   ☐ stems   ☐ rose

2. Label the flower. Use the words in the box.

> stem   bud   ~~petals~~   leaves   roots   seeds

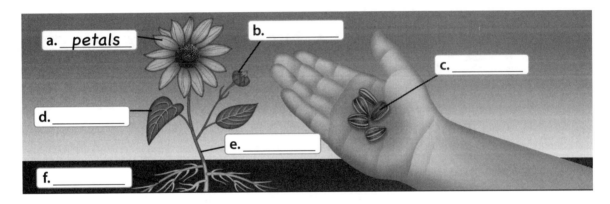

a. _petals_
b. _____
c. _____
d. _____
e. _____
f. _____

3. Read the article and the sentences. Check (✓) the answers.

a. These flowers are for friends.

☐ sunflowers and yellow tulips

☐ yellow roses and sunflowers

b. These flowers are for true love.

☐ red tulips

☐ pink roses

c. These flowers say,
"You're young and beautiful."

☐ white tulips

☐ white rosebuds

Say it with Flowers

Do you know that different flowers say different things? For example, one red rose says, "**I love you**." Pink roses say, "**Thank you**." Here are some flowers and what they mean.

| | GOOD FRIENDS |
Yellow Roses

| | YOUNG AND BEAUTIFUL |
White Rosebuds

| | TRUE LOVE |
Red Tulips

| | TRUE FRIEND |
Sunflowers

Marine Life, Amphibians, and Reptiles

1. **Check (✓) the words you know. Open your dictionary.
   Find the words you don't know.**

   > ## Word List: Marine Life, Amphibians, and Reptiles
   > ### Dictionary page 212
   >
   > ☐ fin   ☐ shark   ☐ swordfish
   > ☐ gills   ☐ tuna   ☐ starfish
   > ☐ scales   ☐ octopus   ☐ frog

2. **Write the words in the chart. Use the words in the box.**

~~shark~~   tuna   octopus   swordfish   starfish   frog

Fins		No Fins	
a.	*shark*	d.	
b.		e.	
c.		f.	

3. **Read the sentences. Circle the correct words.**

   a. A shark /(frog) can live in the water or
      out of the water.

   b. An octopus / A swordfish has eight arms.

   c. A fin / starfish usually has five arms.

   d. A gill / swordfish has a long "nose."

   e. Some sharks / swordfish can eat fish
      or people.

   f. People buy tuna / scales fresh or in cans.

Challenge Name two things in the Word List with gills.
Name two things in the Word List that don't have scales.

212

4. Check (✓) the animals that have feet. Use your dictionary for help.

Word List: Marine Life, Amphibians, and Reptiles
Dictionary page 213

☐ whale   ☐ walrus   ☐ alligator   ☐ lizard

☐ dolphin   ☐ sea lion   ☐ snake   ☐ turtle

5. Cross out the word that doesn't belong.

a. ~~snake~~   dolphin   whale

b. sea lion   alligator   lizard

c. walrus   dolphin   turtle

d. sea lion   snake   whale

e. turtle   sea lion   snake

6. Look at the pictures. Answer the questions.

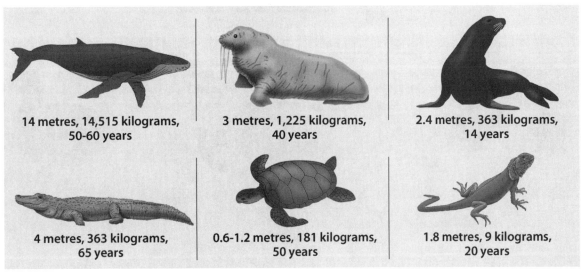

14 metres, 14,515 kilograms, 50-60 years

3 metres, 1,225 kilograms, 40 years

2.4 metres, 363 kilograms, 14 years

4 metres, 363 kilograms, 65 years

0.6-1.2 metres, 181 kilograms, 50 years

1.8 metres, 9 kilograms, 20 years

a. Which animal is short and heavy?   turtle

b. Which animal lives 50–60 years? _____

c. Which reptile is 363 kilograms? _____

d. Which animals live 20 years or less? _____ _____

e. Which animal would you like to be? _____

Birds, Insects, and Arachnids

1. Check (✓) the words you know. Open your dictionary. Find the words you don't know.

Word List: Birds, Insects, and Arachnids
Dictionary page 214

☐ wing   ☐ blue jay   ☐ butterfly

☐ feather   ☐ duck   ☐ (honey)bee

☐ owl   ☐ pigeon   ☐ spider

2. Match the words with the pictures.

1.

2.

3.

4.

5.

6.

_3_ **a.** bee   ___ **c.** spider   ___ **e.** pigeon

___ **b.** duck   ___ **d.** butterfly   ___ **f.** feather

3. Read the sentences. Circle the correct words.

a. (Spiders) / Birds don't have wings.

b. Butterflies / Blue jays have feathers.

c. Ducks / Arachnids are birds.

d. Owls / Bees are insects.

e. Birds and spiders / butterflies have wings.

f. Spiders are arachnids / birds.

1. Check (✓) the animals in your neighbourhood or home.
Use your dictionary for help.

Word List: Domestic Animals and Rodents
Dictionary page 215

☐ cow   ☐ goat   ☐ cat   ☐ mouse

☐ pig   ☐ sheep   ☐ dog   ☐ squirrel

☐ horse   ☐ rooster

2. Unscramble the words.

a. useom   m _o_ _u_ s _e_

b. epesh   s __ __ e __

c. toag   g __ __ t

d. reosh   h __ __ s __

e. sootrer   __ __ __ s t __ r

f. qisurelr   __ q u __ __ __ e __

3. Look at the picture. Circle the correct words.

a. The (cat)/ mouse is sleeping in the sun.

b. The cow / dog is with the sheep.

c. There are three pigs / squirrels.

d. The cow / rooster is eating.

e. The goat / mouse sees the cat.

1. Check (✓) the words you know. Open your dictionary. Find the words you don't know.

Word List: Mammals
Dictionary page 216

☐ coyote	☐ skunk	☐ whiskers
☐ wolf	☐ raccoon	☐ paw
☐ bear	☐ deer	☐ tail

2. Label the pictures. Use the animals in the Word List.

a. _____ *wolf* _____

b. _____

c. _____

d. _____

e. _____

f. _____

3. Look at the animals in the Word List. Read the sentences. Write _T_ (true) or _F_ (false).

a. They all are mammals. _T_

b. They all have tails. ___

c. They all have paws. ___

d. They all have whiskers. ___

e. They all live in Canada. ___

f. They all live far away from people. ___

Challenge Do all mammals have tails?

4. Check (✓) the animals you like to see at the zoo. Use your dictionary for help.

> **Word List: Mammals**
> **Dictionary page 217**
>
> ☐ llama ☐ giraffe ☐ tiger ☐ elephant
> ☐ monkey ☐ zebra ☐ camel ☐ kangaroo
> ☐ gorilla ☐ lion

5. Match the words with the sentences

<u>6</u> **a.** llama   **1.** It lives in trees.

___ **b.** giraffe   **2.** It lives in Australia.

___ **c.** tiger   **3.** It's black and white.

___ **d.** zebra   **4.** It has a very long neck.

___ **e.** kangaroo   **5.** It's a big cat.

___ **f.** monkey   **6.** It lives in South America.

6. Look at the pictures. Check (✓) the correct sentences.

a. ☑ It's a gorilla.

☐ It's a llama.

b. ☐ The camel is thirsty.

☐ Elephants like the water.

c. ☐ Tigers live alone.

☐ Lions live in groups.

d. ☐ Camels live in the desert.

☐ Camels have two paws.

1. **Check (✓) the words you know. Open your dictionary. Find the words you don't know.**

> ### Word List: Energy and Conservation
> #### Dictionary page 218
>
> ☐ solar energy   ☐ coal   ☐ air pollution
>
> ☐ wind power   ☐ oil   ☐ hazardous waste
>
> ☐ natural gas   ☐ nuclear energy   ☐ water pollution

2. **Match the words.**

    __4__ **a.** solar   **1.** pollution

    ____ **b.** air   **2.** waste

    ____ **c.** natural   **3.** gas

    ____ **d.** wind   **4.** energy

    ____ **e.** hazardous   **5.** power

3. **Label the picture. Use the words in the box.**

    > ~~wind power~~   oil   coal   nuclear energy   air pollution   water pollution

a. ___wind power___

b. _____

c. _____

d. _____

e. _____

f. _____

4. Check (✓) the ways you conserve in your home. Use your dictionary for help.

> **Word List: Energy and Conservation**
> Dictionary page 219
>
> ☐ **reduce** trash   ☐ **turn off** lights   ☐ **plant** a tree
> ☐ **recycle**   ☐ **carpool**
> ☐ **save** water   ☐ **don't litter**

5. Complete the words. Write the letters.

a. r _e_ c y _c_ l e

b. __ a r __ o o __

c. s __ v __   w __ t __ __

d. r e __ u __ e   t __ a s __

e. __ __ n't   __ i __ __ e __

f. p __ __ __ t   a   t r __ __

6. Look at the pictures. Circle the correct words.

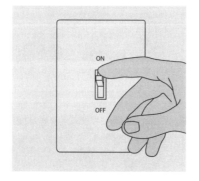

a. Ellen (reduces) / recycles trash.

b. Pablo always turns off the litter / lights.

c. Becca and Norma carpool / don't drive to work.

d. Sue saves water / recycles.

e. Glen recycles / plants a tree every year.

f. John and Kate save water / don't litter.

Canadian National Parks

1. **Check (✓) the words you know. Open your dictionary.**
   Find the words you don't know.

Word List: Canadian National Parks
Dictionary pages 220-221

☐ landmarks   ☐ wildlife   ☐ landscape   ☐ **take** a tour

☐ park ranger   ☐ ferry   ☐ cave

2. **Label the pictures. Use the words in the Word List.**

a. _____landmark_____   b. _____   c. _____

d. _____   e. _____   f. _____

g. _____

3. Read the story. Circle the correct words.

a. National parks are home to a variety of rangers / (wildlife.)

b. At some parks you can take a landmark / tour.

c. Some parks have caves / national parks.

d. You can get to some parks by landmark / ferry.

e. National ferries / parks have park rangers.

f. The wildlife / park rangers can answer your questions.

4. What about you? Answer the questions. Write *Yes* or *No*.

a. Does your province have many national parks?_____

b. Do you like to visit parks? _____

c. Would you like to be a park ranger? _____

Challenge Name a national park you want to visit.

1. Check (✓) the places you like. Use your dictionary for help.

Word List: Places to Go
Dictionary pages 222–223

- ☐ zoo
- ☐ movies
- ☐ botanical garden
- ☐ bowling alley
- ☐ rock concert

- ☐ swap meet
- ☐ aquarium
- ☐ play
- ☐ art gallery
- ☐ amusement park

- ☐ opera
- ☐ nightclub
- ☐ county fair
- ☐ classical concert

2. Cross out the word that doesn't belong.

a. ~~nightclub~~	zoo	botanical garden
b. movie	play	swap meet
c. aquarium	nightclub	zoo
d. county fair	classical concert	opera
e. amusement park	museum	bowling alley
f. rock concert	movie	classical concert

3. Match the words with the pictures.

1. zoo
2. classical concert
3. aquarium

4. swap meet
5. botanical garden
6. nightclub

_1_ a.    b.    c.

___ d.    e.    f.

4. Label the picture. Use the words in the box.

| ~~nightclub~~ | bowling alley | movies | opera | rock concert |

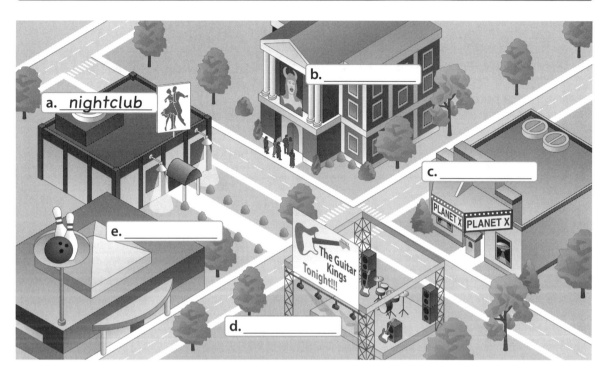

a. _nightclub_

b. _____

c. _____

d. _____

e. _____

The Guitar Kings Tonight!!!

PLANET X   PLANET X

5. Read the ads. Answer the questions.

a. How many concerts are there?   _____2_____

b. What type of concert is Mozart's Best?   _____

c. What's the name of the play?   _____

d. How much is the rock concert?   _____

e. Is there an amusement park?   _____

f. Where can you see fish and other sea animals?   _____

223

1. Check (✓) the words you know. Open your dictionary. Find the words you don't know.

Word List: The Park and Playground
Dictionary page 224

☐ bike path   ☐ slide   ☐ **climb** the bars
☐ tennis court   ☐ **pull** the wagon ☐ **have** a picnic
☐ bench   ☐ **push** the swing

2. Match the words.

_5_ **a.** push   **1.** the bars

___ **b.** play tennis   **2.** the wagon

___ **c.** sit   **3.** on the bike path

___ **d.** climb   **4.** on the tennis court

___ **e.** pull   **5.** the swing

___ **f.** ride a bike   **6.** on the bench

3. Label the picture. Use the words in the box.

~~swings~~   slide   bench   picnic   wagon   bars

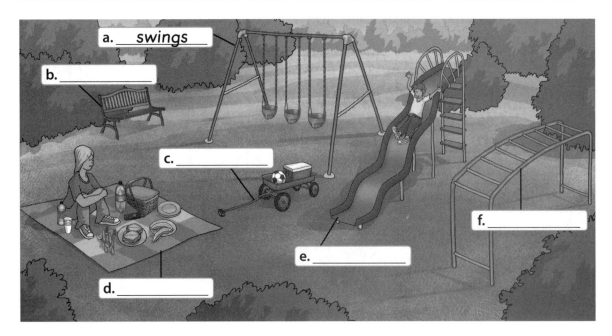

a. ___swings___

b. _____

c. _____

d. _____

e. _____

f. _____

See page 309 for listening practice.

1. Check (✓) the things people bring to the beach. Use your dictionary for help.

> **Word List: The Beach**
> Dictionary page 225
>
> ☐ ocean   ☐ surfboard   ☐ lifeguard
> ☐ sandcastle   ☐ wave   ☐ beach chair
> ☐ beach umbrella   ☐ pier   ☐ sand

2. Unscramble the sentences.

a. ocean is The blue. _The ocean is blue._____

b. The large. are waves _____

c. the pier. is The lifeguard on _____

d. a We're sandcastle. making _____

e. the beach. There's sand at _____

3. Look at the picture. Read the sentences. Number the people.

1. Paul has a surfboard.

2. Lou is a lifeguard.

3. Erika is making a sandcastle.

4. Marta is sitting in a beach chair.

5. Ray is in the ocean.

6. Grace has a beach umbrella.

1. Check (✓) the words you know. Open your dictionary.
   Find the words you don't know.

> ### Word List: Outdoor Recreation
> #### Dictionary page 226
>
> ☐ fishing   ☐ tent   ☐ backpack
>
> ☐ camping   ☐ sleeping bag   ☐ fishing pole
>
> ☐ hiking   ☐ life vest   ☐ canteen

2. Read the sentences. Circle the correct words.

   a. Use a tent for (camping)/ fishing.

   b. Use a life vest for <u>hiking / fishing</u>.

   c. Put water in a <u>canteen / sleeping bag</u>.

   d. A backpack is good for <u>hiking / fishing</u>.

   e. Use a <u>tent / fishing</u> pole for fishing.

   f. Camping, fishing, and hiking are types of outdoor <u>recreation / life vests</u>.

3. Read the ad. Answer the questions.

   a. How much is the fishing pole? $64.99

   b. How much is the backpack?   _____

   c. How much are the tents?   _____

   d. Jack buys a fishing pole and a backpack.
         The tax is $10.04. What is the total?   _____

Challenge Look at the ad in Exercise 3. What type of store is this?

1. **Check (✓) the sports you like. Use your dictionary for help.**

> ### Word List: Winter and Water Sports
> #### Dictionary page 227
>
> ☐ skiing ☐ ice skating ☐ sailing ☐ snorkelling
> ☐ snowboarding ☐ water skiing ☐ surfing ☐ scuba diving

2. **Cross out the word that doesn't belong.**

a.	waterskiing	~~ice skating~~	snorkelling
b.	surfing	sailing	winter sports
c.	snowboarding	skiing	snorkelling
d.	snorkelling	sailing	scuba diving
e.	ice skating	skiing	water sports

3. **Look at the pictures. Circle the correct words.**

a. He likes water skiing / (scuba diving).

b. She likes snorkelling / skiing.

c. She likes winter / water sports.

d. She really likes sailing / surfing.

e. She likes winter / water sports.

f. Her favourite sport is
skiing / snowboarding.

1. **Check (✓) the things you like to watch. Use your dictionary for help.**

Word List: Individual Sports
Dictionary page 228

☐ bowling   ☐ golf   ☐ tennis

☐ boxing   ☐ gymnastics   ☐ track and field

☐ cycling   ☐ skateboarding

2. **Match the words with the pictures.**

1.    2.   3.   4.   5.

__5__ **a.** boxing   ____ **c.** skateboarding   ____ **e.** bowling

____ **b.** golf   ____ **d.** track and field

3. **Label the pictures. Use the words in the box.**

golf   ~~boxing~~   gymnastics   cycling   tennis   skateboarding

a. _____*boxing*_____   b. _____   c. _____

d. _____   e. _____   f. _____

Challenge Name three individual sports that can be dangerous.

1. **Check (✓) the words you know. Open your dictionary. Find the words you don't know.**

   > **Word List: Team Sports**
   > **Dictionary page 229**
   >
   > ☐ score   ☐ baseball
   > ☐ coach   ☐ football
   > ☐ player   ☐ soccer
   > ☐ official   ☐ hockey
   > ☐ basketball   ☐ volleyball

2. **Complete the words. Write the letters.**

   a. p _l_ a _y_ _e_ r   d. s c ___ ___ ___

   b. c ___ ___ c h   e. ___ o l l ___ ___ b ___ l l

   c. s ___ c c ___ ___   f. o ___ ___ i c ___ ___ l

3. **Study the graph. Answer the questions.**

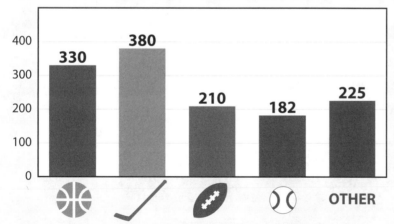

What Sports Do People Like to Watch?

330 380 210 182 225

   a. What is the favourite sport to watch?   _hockey_

   b. How many people like to watch basketball?   _____

   c. How many people like to watch football?   _____

   d. How many people like baseball?   _____

   e. Name three "other" sports.   _____ _____ _____

Sports Verbs

1. **Check (✓) the things you can do. Use your dictionary for help.**

Word List: Sports Verbs
Dictionary page 230

☐ pitch	☐ catch	☐ shoot	☐ dive
☐ hit	☐ kick	☐ jump	☐ stretch
☐ throw	☐ pass		

2. **Unscramble the words.**

a. sasp   p _a_ _s_ s

b. thoso   sh __ __ t

c. ikkc   k __ __ __

d. veid   __ __ v __

e. thicp   p __ __ c __

f. whrot   __ __ r o __

g. pumj   __ __ __ p

h. chertts   __ t __ __ __ c h

3. **Label the pictures. Use the words in the box.**

throw	~~jump~~	catch	pitch	hit	stretch

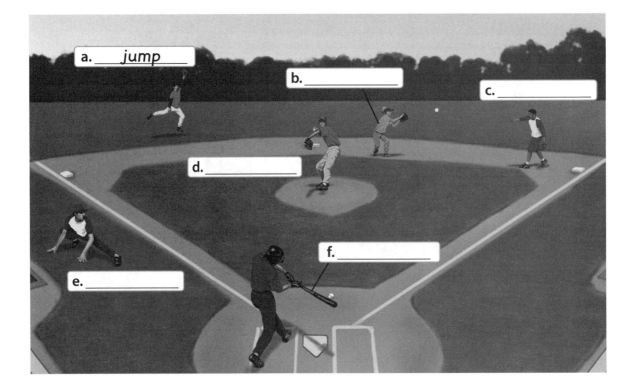

a. _jump_

b. _____

c. _____

d. _____

e. _____

f. _____

Challenge Look at the picture in Exercise 3. What sport are they playing?

1. Check (✓) the things you have at home. Use your dictionary for help.

Word List: Sports Equipment
Dictionary page 231

- ☐ golf club
- ☐ tennis racket
- ☐ volleyball
- ☐ basketball
- ☐ bowling ball
- ☐ soccer ball
- ☐ baseball bat
- ☐ uniform
- ☐ baseball
- ☐ football

2. Match the words with the pictures.

_5_ **a.** tennis racket
____ **b.** football
____ **c.** baseball
____ **d.** basketball
____ **e.** volleyball
____ **f.** uniform

1.
2.
3.
4.
5.
6.

3. Complete the crossword puzzle.

ACROSS

2. bowling _____
4. _____ equipment
5. tennis _____

DOWN

1. golf _____
2. baseball _____
3. _____ ball

					1
			2 B	A	L	L
		3			
4					
5					

1. **Check (✓) the words you know. Open your dictionary.
Find the words you don't know.**

Word List: Hobbies and Games
Dictionary pages 232-233

☐ **play** games   ☐ board game   ☐ oil paint
☐ **paint**   ☐ dice   ☐ paintbrush
☐ **knit**   ☐ checkers   ☐ watercolour
☐ **play** cards   ☐ chess   ☐ yarn
☐ video game console   ☐ canvas   ☐ knitting needles

2. **Write the words in the chart. Use all the words in the Word List.**

Game Words		Hobby Words	
a.	play games	h.	
b.		i.	
c.		j.	
d.		k.	
e.		l.	
f.		m.	
g.		n.	
		o.	

3. **Read the sentences. Write *T* (true) or *F* (false).**

a. You can paint with watercolours.   _T_

b. You need two knitting needles and yarn to knit.   ___

c. Chess and cards are board games.   ___

d. You need construction paper for embroidery   ___

e. You need two dice for checkers.   ___

f. You need a TV or a computer for video games.   ___

4. Look at the picture. Circle the correct words.

a. Today is Thanksgiving. We're playing hobbies / (games) and having fun.

b. My brothers are playing cards / chess.

c. Our friends are playing a board / paint game.

d. My cousin and I are playing our favourite dice / video game.

e. Grandma is painting / knitting. It's her favourite canvas / hobby.

5. Study the graph. Answer the questions.

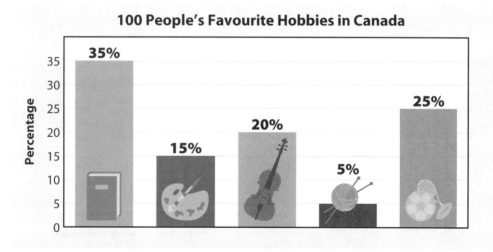

a. What percent of people like to read? _____35%_____

b. What percent like to knit? _____

c. What percent like to paint? _____

d. What is the number one hobby? _____

Electronics and Photography

1. **Check (✓) the things you have at home. Use your dictionary for help.**

> ### Word List: Electronics and Photography
> #### Dictionary page 234
>
> ☐ CD boom box   ☐ headphones   ☐ DVD player
>
> ☐ MP3 player   ☐ flat screen TV   ☐ speakers
>
> ☐ dock   ☐ universal remote

2. **Complete the words. Write the letters.**

   a. r _e_ m o _t_ e

   b. d ___ ___ ___

   c. D ___ D   p ___ ___ y e ___

   d. ___ ___ e a ___ e r s

   e. h ___ ___ d ___ h o ___ e s

   f. ___ D   b ___ ___ ___ ___   b ___ ___

3. **Label the pictures. Use the words in the box.**

DVD player	~~CD boom box~~	speakers	remote
MP3 player	headphones	flat screen TV	

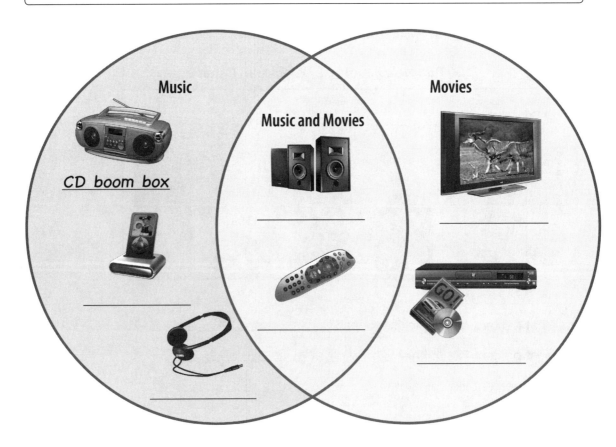

Music

Movies

Music and Movies

CD boom box

4. Check (✓) the words you know. Open your dictionary. Find the words you don't know.

> **Word List: Electronics and Photography**
> **Dictionary page 235**
>
> ☐ digital camera   ☐ battery pack   ☐ **rewind**
> ☐ memory card   ☐ **record**   ☐ **fast forward**
> ☐ camcorder   ☐ **play**   ☐ **pause**

5. Match the words.

<u>2</u> **a.** battery   **1.** forward

___ **b.** memory   **2.** pack

___ **c.** fast   **3.** card

___ **d.** digital   **4.** the movie

___ **e.** play   **5.** camera

6. Look at the pictures. Put the sentences in order (1–6).

___ They record their day at the park.

___ They pause the tape and make popcorn.

<u>1</u> The Adani family has a new digital camcorder.

___ Now the children are tired. They fast forward to the end.

___ They play the family movie on their TV.

___ They rewind the funny parts and watch them again.

1. Check (✓) programs you watch. Use your dictionary for help.

> **Word List: Entertainment**
> Dictionary page 236
>
> ☐ news program   ☐ talk show   ☐ game show
> ☐ sitcom   ☐ soap opera   ☐ sports program
> ☐ cartoon   ☐ reality show   ☐ drama

2. Match the words with the sentences.

_5_ **a.** news program   **1.** It's for kids.

___ **b.** sitcom   **2.** It's funny.

___ **c.** drama   **3.** It's serious.

___ **d.** sports program   **4.** It shows football, baseball, or other sports.

___ **e.** cartoon   **5.** It tells you about the world.

3. Look at the pictures. Write T (true) or F (false).

a. It's a news program. _T_   **b.** It's a reality show. ___   **c.** It's a soap opera. ___

 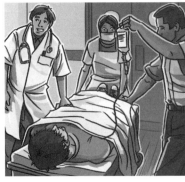 

d. It's a talk show. ___   **e.** It's a game show. ___   **f.** It's a sitcom. ___

4. Check (✓) the movies and music you like. Use your dictionary. Find the words you don't know.

Word List: Entertainment
Dictionary page 237

Types of Movies
- ☐ comedy
- ☐ tragedy
- ☐ action
- ☐ mystery

Types of Music
- ☐ classical
- ☐ blues
- ☐ rock
- ☐ jazz
- ☐ pop

5. Cross out the word that doesn't belong.

a. jazz   ~~action~~   blues

b. comedy   action   classical

c. tragedy   pop   classical

d. rock   pop   movies

e. music   action   mystery

6. Label the movie posters. Use the words in the box.

| comedy | tragedy | action | mystery |

a. _____   **b.** _____   **c.** _____   **d.** _____

Music

1. Check (✓) the words you know. Open your dictionary. Find the words you don't know.

> ### Word List: Music
> #### Dictionary page 238
>
> ☐ **play** an instrument   ☐ clarinet   ☐ trumpet
>
> ☐ **sing** a song   ☐ violin   ☐ piano
>
> ☐ flute   ☐ guitar   ☐ drums

2. Match the words with the pictures.

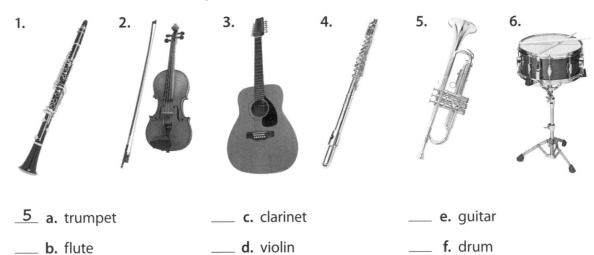

1.   2.   3.   4.   5.   6.

__5__ **a.** trumpet   ____ **c.** clarinet   ____ **e.** guitar

____ **b.** flute   ____ **d.** violin   ____ **f.** drum

3. Look at the picture. Read the sentences. Number the people.

1. Jim plays the guitar.
2. Ella sings the songs.
3. Matt plays the drums.
4. Scott plays the piano.
5. Miles plays the trumpet.

a. __3__

b. ____

c. ____

d. ____

e. ____

Challenge Do you play an instrument?

1. Check (✓) the words you know. Open your dictionary. Find the words you don't know.

> **Word List: Holidays**
> **Dictionary page 239**
>
> ☐ parade   ☐ mask   ☐ feast
> ☐ fireworks   ☐ jack-o'-lantern   ☐ ornament
> ☐ flag   ☐ costume   ☐ Christmas tree

2. Unscramble the words.

a. readap   p _a_ r a _d_ e   **d.** stafe   f ___ ___ s ___

b. fgla   f ___ ___ ___   **e.** cemtosu   c ___ ___ t ___ ___ e

c. ksam   m ___ ___ ___   **f.** kerifsrow   ___ ___ r e ___ o r ___ ___

3. Label the pictures. Write the numbers.

1. costume
2. ornament
3. fireworks
4. ~~mask~~
5. parade
6. Christmas tree
7. flag
8. jack-o'-lantern

Challenge Name a holiday that has fireworks. Name a holiday that has a parade.

A Birthday Party

1. **Check (✓) the words you know. Open your dictionary.**
   Find the words you don't know.

Word List: Birthday Party
Dictionary pages 240-241

   ☐ decorations   ☐ **videotape**   ☐ **hide**

   ☐ deck   ☐ **make** a wish   ☐ **bring**

   ☐ present   ☐ **blow out**   ☐ **wrap**

2. **Label the pictures. Complete the sentences. Use the words in the box.**

   ~~Wrap~~   videotape   present   deck   balloons   Blow out

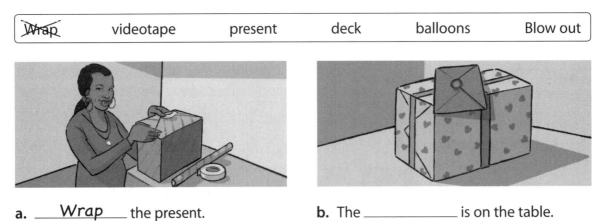

a. ___Wrap___ the present.

b. The _____ is on the table.

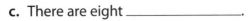

c. There are eight _____.

d. The woman is on the _____.

e. _____ the candles.

f. We always _____ family parties.

3. Read the story. Circle the correct words.

a. Today is Ramon's (birthday) / present.

b. There are many decks / decorations in the yard.

c. There's a present / wish for Ramon on the deck.

d. Right now Ramon is hiding / making a wish.

e. Then he will wrap / blow out the candles.

f. Ramon's wife is videotaping / making the party.

g. His son is hiding / bringing.

h. Ramon is having a great time at his decorations / party.

4. What about you? Answer the questions. Answer *Yes, I do* or *No, I don't*.

a. Do you like birthday parties? _____.

b. Do you like to give presents to people? _____.

c. Do you like to videotape parties and special events? _____.

Look at the picture. There are more than five items that begin with the letter *p*. Find and circle them. Use your dictionary pages 2–29 for help.

**Label the pictures. Use the words in the box. Then find the words in the puzzle.
Use your dictionary pages 30–45 for help.**

tall	~~hungry~~	grandmother	children	exercise
bottle	curly	drive	graduate	toddler

a. _hungry_

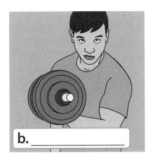

b. _____

c. _____

d. _____

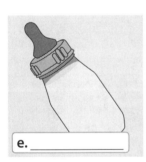

e. _____

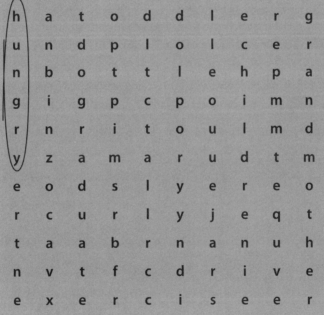

h	a	t	o	d	d	l	e	r	g
u	n	d	p	l	o	l	c	e	r
n	b	o	t	t	l	e	h	p	a
g	i	g	p	c	p	o	i	m	n
r	n	r	i	t	o	u	l	m	d
y	z	a	m	a	r	u	d	t	m
e	o	d	s	l	y	e	r	e	o
r	c	u	r	l	y	j	e	q	t
t	a	a	b	r	n	a	n	u	h
n	v	t	f	c	d	r	i	v	e
e	x	e	r	c	i	s	e	e	r

f. _____

g. _____

h. _____

i. _____

j. _____

243

Read the sentences. Complete the picture. Use your dictionary pages 46–65 for help.

a. There's a sofa in the living room.

b. There's a coffee table in front of the sofa.

c. There are two chairs and a table in the kitchen.

d. There's a flower bed in the yard.

e. There's a dresser in the bedroom.

f. There's a shower in the bathroom.

Circle 10 things in the picture from Unit 4. Then write the words below the picture. Use your dictionary pages 66–85 for help.

oranges _____ _____ _____ _____

_____ _____ _____ _____ _____

Read the words. Look at the pictures. Circle the clothes and accessories you see. Use your dictionary pages 86–103 for help.

a.

blouse
tie

briefcase

b.

sweatpants
T-shirt
shorts

c.

watch
necklace
earrings

d.

evening gown
tuxedo
short skirt

e.

overalls
knit top
sandals

f.

lab coat
robe
pyjamas

Label the pictures. Use the words in the box. Then find the words in the puzzle. Use your dictionary pages 104–123 for help.

arm	eye	doctor	headache	heart
mouth	nose	~~nurse~~	toe	toothbrush

a. _____nurse_____

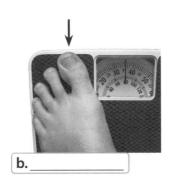

b. _____

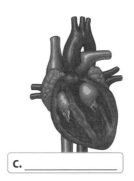

c. _____

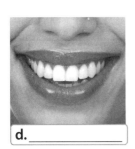

d. _____

```
t  o  o  t  h  b  r  u  s  h
o  v  n  e  e  y  e  n  h  e
a  m  r  e  a  u  m  d  u  a
f  a  n  u  r  s  e  y  o  d
p  d  o  c  t  o  r  e  l  a
a  r  s  r  r  a  y  r  d  c
r  a  e  s  i  m  o  u  t  h
m  r  m  t  e  i  n  t  o  e
```

e. _____

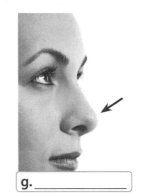

g. _____

f. _____

h. _____

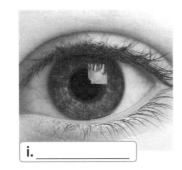

i. _____

j. _____

247

Read the sentences. Complete the picture. Use your dictionary pages 124–149 for help.

a. There's a coffee shop next to the bookstore.

b. There's a pedestrian in the crosswalk.

c. There's a mailbox next to the bus stop.

d. There's a bus in the street.

e. There's a police officer on the corner.

f. There's litter on the sidewalk.

What's wrong with the picture? Complete the sentences. Use the words in the box. Use your dictionary pages 150–163 for help.

| speed limit | motorcycle | tires | car | ~~bicycle~~ | trunk | taxi | helicopter |

a. The ___bicycle___ is on the building.

b. The _____ is on the street.

c. The _____ is in the air.

d. The _____ sign says 150.

e. The _____ is on the sidewalk.

f. The _____ is turning right.

g. The minivan has no _____.

h. The _____ of the convertible is open.

Another Look (Unit 9)

Label the pictures. Use the words in the box. Then find the words in the puzzle. Use your dictionary pages 164–187 for help.

cashier	paycheque	gardener	tools	~~construction~~
nurse	resume	interview	office	factory

b. _____

c. _____

d. _____

a. _construction_

e. _____

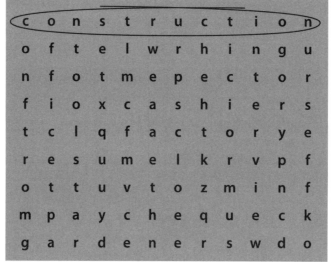

```
c o n s t r u c t i o n
o f t e l w r h i n g u
n f o t m e p e c t o r
f i o x c a s h i e r s
t c l q f a c t o r y e
r e s u m e l k r v p f
o t t u v t o z m i n f
m p a y c h e q u e c k
g a r d e n e r s w d o
```

f. _____

g. _____

h. _____

i. _____

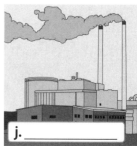

j. _____

Circle 10 things in the picture from Unit 10. Then write the words below the picture. Use your dictionary pages 188–207 for help.

North America

Pacific Ocean

Today is March 12.

Periodic Table of **Elements**

_____ *printer* _____   _____   _____   _____

_____   _____   _____   _____

_____   _____

Another Look (Unit 11)

What's wrong with the picture? Complete the sentences. Use the words in the box. Use your dictionary pages 208–221 for help.

| wings | ~~dolphin~~ | palm tree | pig | swordfish | nest |

a. There's a ___*dolphin*___ in the lake.

b. There's snow on the _____.

c. A _____ is drinking from the lake.

d. The dog is sitting on a _____.

e. The frog has _____.

f. There's a _____ in the tree.

252

Circle 10 things in the picture from Unit 12. Then write the words below the picture. Use your dictionary pages 222–241 for help.

paintbrush _____ _____ _____ _____

_____ _____ _____ _____

LISTENING
EXERCISES

Oxford Picture Dictionary p. 4

🎧 1. Listen to the entire conversation. Answer the questions with your class.

    a. Where is Carlos?

    b. What is he doing?

🎧 2. Listen to each part of the conversation. Underline the words you hear.

> **a.** Can you (spell / say) that for me, please?
>
> **b.** Is there (an apartment / a street) number with that?
>
> **c.** What (province / city) do you live in?
>
> **d.** Now I need your (phone / cell) number.
>
> **e.** And what's your (birthplace / date of birth)?
>
> **f.** Put your (social insurance number / signature) right there.

🎧 3. Listen again. Complete the form.

School Registration Form

first name		last name	
_ _ _ _ Maple St., **address**	# 3B **apartment number**	London **city**	
Ontario **province**	**postal code**	(_ _ _ _)_ _ _ _-_ _ _ _ _ **phone number**	**cell phone number**
San Jose, Costa Rica **birthplace**	10/ /1985 **DOB**	900-_ _ _-_ _ _ **SIN**	M F **sex**

4. Complete the form with your own information.

address	**apartment number**	**city**
province	**postal code**	

🎧 1. Look at the picture at the top of pages 6 and 7 in the OPD. Listen to the entire conversation. Answer the questions with your class.

    a. What is Tom looking for?

    b. How many people does he ask for help?

    c. Does he find it?

🎧 2. Close your book. Listen to each part of the conversation. Underline the words you hear.

> **a.** I think it's over there by the (desk / computer).
>
> **b.** Well, look in the (bookcase / desk).
>
> **c.** He's over there, in front of the (clock / map).
>
> **d.** It's on her (chair / desk).
>
> **e.** It's near her (notebook / textbook).
>
> **f.** The teacher is at the (map / projector)

🎧 3. Check (✓) the words you heard. Then listen again and check your answers.

☐ dictionary	☐ pencil	☐ textbooks	☐ workbooks
☐ pen	☐ listening	☐ headphones	☐ talking
☐ sit down	☐ open	☐ stand up	☐ students

4. List the things you see in your classroom and on your desk.

Classroom	Desk
clock	*pens*

Oxford Picture Dictionary p. 13

🎧 1. Look at the weather map on page 13 in the OPD. Listen to the entire forecast. Answer the questions with your class.

   a. What five places are in the forecast?

   _____

   _____

   b. Which place is hot?

   _____

   c. Which place is cold?

   _____

🎧 2. Close your book. Listen to each part of the forecast. Underline *True* or *False*.

a. It's sunny in Toronto.	True	False
b. It's warm in Calgary.	True	False
c. It's raining in Vancouver.	True	False
d. It's snowing in Montreal.	True	False

🎧 3. Check (✓) the words you heard. Then listen again and check your answers.

☐ clear	☐ heat wave	☐ windy	☐ cool
☐ freezing	☐ raining	☐ foggy	☐ thunderstorm
☐ snowing	☐ warm	☐ snowstorm	☐ hot

4. Write about the weather in your area.

   Today the weather is _____ .

   Today the temperature is _____ .

   Yesterday the temperature was _____ .

   Last week the weather was _____ .

🎧 **1.** Listen to the commentators on the recording. Answer the questions with your class.

    a. What event is taking place?

    b. When is it taking place?

🎧 **2.** Listen to each part of the conversation. Underline the words you hear.

> **a.** What a beautiful day here — (ninety / nineteen) degrees and sunny.
>
> **b.** This morning he placed (fifth / first) in both the 100-metre and 200-metre races.
>
> **c.** We'll return at (one / nine) o'clock.

🎧 **3.** Listen again. Check (✔) the words you hear.

☐ thirtieth	☐ zero	☐ eighth	☐ ninth
☐ forty-nine	☐ twelve	☐ twenty-three	☐ ten
☐ eleven	☐ sixty	☐ one hundred	☐ ninetieth

4. Write the words you checked in exercise 3 in the chart below.

Cardinal Numbers	Ordinal Numbers

Oxford Picture Dictionary p. 22

1. Listen to the entire conversation. Answer the questions with your class.

    a. What is the couple talking about?

    b. What does the couple decide to do?

2. Listen to each part of the conversation. Underline the words you hear.

> a. We should start planning our next (vacation / birthday) soon, dear.
>
> b. You mean we wouldn't be home for (Good Friday / Thanksgiving) or my birthday?
>
> c. We can't miss the (appointment / wedding)!
>
> d. We can spend (Christmas / Canada Day) there.

3. Check (✓) the words you heard. Then listen again and check your answers.

> ☐ anniversary ☐ appointment ☐ religious holiday ☐ Boxing Day
> ☐ Thanksgiving ☐ New Year's Day ☐ parent-teacher conference ☐ Victoria Day
> ☐ vacation ☐ wedding ☐ Labour Day ☐ Canada Day

4. Write short answers.

    a. Which holidays do you celebrate?

_____

_____

    b. What is your favourite holiday?

_____

_____

    c. Where do you like to go on vacation?

_____

_____

🎧 **1.** Listen to the conversations. Answer the questions with your class.

    a. Where are the conversations taking place?

    b. How many customers does the vendor have?

🎧 **2.** Listen to each part of the conversation. Underline the words you hear.

> **a.** Here's your change: a five, a (loonie / toonie), and a quarter.
>
> **b.** Three dollars and (five / ten) cents, please.
>
> **c.** I've got...a toonie, two loonies, six (quarters / dimes), three nickels, and seven pennies.
>
> **d.** Here you go — three (dollars / cents).

🎧 **3.** Listen again. How much money did each customer give to the vendor? Complete the chart.

Customer	Amount of money given to the vendor	Amount of change gotten back
1		
2		
4		
4		

4. Look at the amounts you wrote in the second column of the chart in C. Choose one of the amounts and write down three different combinations of bills and coins that add up to that amount.

Oxford Picture Dictionary p. 27

🎧 1. Listen to all four conversations between the clerk and her customers. Answer the questions with your class.

   a. What does this store sell?

   b. What do the customers want to do?

🎧 2. Listen to each conversation. Underline the words you hear.

---

a. I want to (exchange / return) this lamp.

b. I want to pay with a (personal cheque / debit card).

c. The (sale price / sales tax) for this lamp is $12.50.

d. I want to (exchange / return) this lamp.

🎧 3. Check (✓) the words you heard. Then listen again and check your answers.

☐ exchange   ☐ buy   ☐ debit card   ☐ pay

☐ credit card   ☐ total   ☐ write   ☐ sales tax

☐ gift card   ☐ return   ☐ receipt   ☐ traveller's cheque

---

4. Write the appropriate words from exercise 3 in the chart.

Ways to Pay

Oxford Picture Dictionary p. 32

🎧 **1.** Listen to the entire conversation. Answer the questions with your class.

    a. What does the woman ask Nishad to do?

    b. How does she try to help him?

🎧 **2.** Listen to each part of the conversation. Underline the words you hear.

> **a.** Just look for three (tall / attractive) young women.
>
> **b.** Well, Meghan is short and (thin / elderly).
>
> **c.** Wow, that is (tall / heavy)
>
> **d.** Oh, she's (short / an average height), like me.

🎧 **3.** Check (✔) the words you heard. Then listen again and check your answers.

> ☐ tall   ☐ average weight   ☐ pierced ear   ☐ tattoo
>
> ☐ cute   ☐ pregnant   ☐ young   ☐ elderly
>
> ☐ fat   ☐ attractive   ☐ physically challenged   ☐ mole

    4. Write a short description of yourself using the words from page 32 in the OPD.

_____

_____

_____

_____

_____

Oxford Picture Dictionary pp. 34–35

🎧 1. Look at pages 34 and 35 in the OPD. Listen to the entire conversation. Answer the questions with your class.

    a. Who is talking to Sue?

    b. What is happening tonight?

🎧 2. Listen to each part of the conversation. Underline the words you hear.

> **a.** My (wife's / sister's) family is coming over tonight.
>
> **b.** My (mother / brother)-in-law and father-in-law are coming.
>
> **c.** My (son / daughter) is 12.
>
> **d.** My brother-in-law and (father / sister)-in-law are coming.
>
> **e.** My (nephew / niece) is 6.
>
> **f.** My (daughter / wife) is cleaning the house.

🎧 3. Check (✓) the words you heard. Then listen again and check your answers.

> ☐ mother-in-law   ☐ uncle   ☐ nephew   ☐ aunt
>
> ☐ children   ☐ niece   ☐ grandparents   ☐ daughter
>
> ☐ cousins   ☐ grandmother   ☐ son   ☐ grandfather

4. Look at page 34 in the OPD. Fill in the blanks with the names of Ana Garcia's family members.

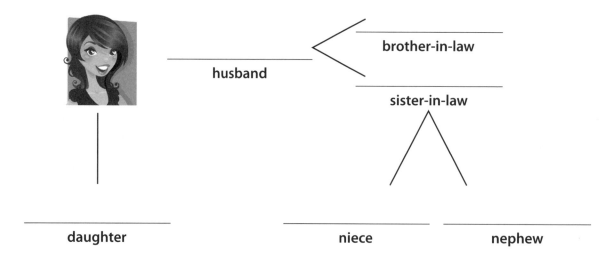

husband   brother-in-law

sister-in-law

daughter   niece   nephew

Oxford Picture Dictionary pp. 36–37

🎧 **1.** Listen to the entire conversation between a husband and a wife. Answer the questions with your class.

    a. Why is the woman leaving?

    b. Who is staying with the baby?

    c. How does the mother feel? How does the father feel?

🎧 **2.** Listen to each part of the conversation. Underline the words you hear.

> **a.** Don't forget to (bathe / feed) Joey tonight.
>
> **b.** There are (bibs / diapers) on the table.
>
> **c.** Don't (feed / rock) him until 3:00, though.
>
> **d.** Be sure you have (diapers / wipes) if you take him out.
>
> **e.** Take the (car safety seat / stroller).
>
> **f.** (Rock / Play with) him before bed.

🎧 **3.** Check (✓) the words you heard. Then listen again and check your answers.

> ☐ bathe   ☐ formula   ☐ buckle up   ☐ diapers
>
> ☐ bib   ☐ stroller   ☐ bottle   ☐ baby bag
>
> ☐ rock   ☐ baby food   ☐ play   ☐ sing

4. Write the words you checked in exercise 3 in the chart.

Actions	Things
bathe	

Oxford Picture Dictionary pp. 38–39

🎧 1. Look at pages 38 and 39 in the OPD. Listen to the story. Point to the times you hear. Answer the question with your class. Who is telling the story?

🎧 2. Close your book. Listen to each part of the story. Underline the times you hear.

---

a. At my house, we eat breakfast together at (7:00 / 7:30).

b. My parents take us to school at (7:30 / 8:30).

c. My mom picks us up from school at (4:00 / 5:00).

d. After dinner, usually around (6:30 / 7:30), my sister and I do homework.

e. At (8:00 / 9:00), I'm still working hard on my homework.

f. About (8:00 / 8:30), my sister and I go to bed.

🎧 3. Check (✓) the words you heard. Then listen again and check your answers.

☐ takes the bus	☐ do homework	☐ exercise	☐ drives
☐ get dressed	☐ reads the paper	☐ clean the house	☐ get up
☐ watches TV	☐ take a shower	☐ relax	☐ checks email

---

4. List six things you do every day.

_____

_____

_____

_____

_____

_____

🎧 **1.** Look at pages 40 and 41 in the OPD. Listen to two people talk about family photos. Answer the questions with your class.

    a. Who is the woman who is speaking?

    b. Who is the man who is speaking?

    c. Where was Grandfather born?

🎧 **2.** Close your book. Listen to each part of the conversation. Underline the years you hear.

> **a.** We went to Egypt in (2005 / 2006).
>
> **b.** He was born in (1945 / 1935), two years before me.
>
> **c.** He immigrated with his parents in (1950 / 1960).
>
> **d.** He graduated in (1963 / 1953).
>
> **e.** He got his degree in (1949 / 1959).
>
> **f.** No, we bought this house in (1965 / 1956).

🎧 **3.** Check (✓) the words you heard. Then listen again and check your answers.

> ☐ retired   ☐ immigrated   ☐ fell in love   ☐ volunteered
>
> ☐ became a citizen   ☐ get married   ☐ travelled   ☐ graduated
>
> ☐ bought this house   ☐ was born   ☐ had a baby   ☐ died

    4. Make a timeline for your life. Include significant years in your life and a brief description of each.

_____   _____

_____   _____

_____   _____

_____   _____

_____   _____

_____   _____

Oxford Picture Dictionary pp. 42–43

🎧 **1.** Listen to the entire conversation. Answer the questions with your class.

    a. Why hasn't Riyaad been studying for his exam?

    b. What advice does Danny give Riyaad?

🎧 **2.** Listen to each part of the conversation. Underline the words you hear.

> **a.** You always help me out when I'm (embarrassed / confused) by the professor.
>
> **b.** I met someone last week and I think I'm (in pain / in love)!
>
> **c.** You're (upset / excited) over nothing.
>
> **d.** You didn't have to be (afraid / disgusted) to ask her out.
>
> **e.** I can concentrate better when I'm (sleepy / full).

🎧 **3.** Check (✓) the words you heard. Then listen again and check your answers.

☐ frustrated	☐ uncomfortable	☐ thirsty	☐ hungry
☐ bored	☐ confused	☐ surprised	☐ proud
☐ upset	☐ lonely	☐ excited	☐ cold

4. Choose three words from exercise 3. What might cause someone to have these feelings? Complete the chart.

Feeling	Causes

🎧 **1.** Listen to the entire conversation. Answer the questions with your class.

    a. What is Mrs. Denunzio doing?

    b. Does she mention anything that she doesn't like?

🎧 **2.** Listen to each part of the conversation. Underline the words you hear.

> **a.** Your (classified ad / furnished apartment) said that the apartment is 800 dollars a month.
>
> **b.** Are (internet listings / utilities) included?
>
> **c.** Hmm, I would have to (unpack / paint) this room.
>
> **d.** First, I'll need you to (submit an application / ask about the features).
>
> **e.** I'll start (packing / meeting the neighbours) today.

🎧 **3.** Check (✔) the words you heard. Then listen again and check your answers.

> ☐ unfurnished apartment   ☐ call the manager   ☐ utilities
>
> ☐ furnished apartment   ☐ submit an application   ☐ move in
>
> ☐ sign the rental agreement   ☐ look at houses   ☐ classified ad
>
> ☐ pay the first and last months' rent   ☐ make a mortgage payment   ☐ meet the neighbours

4. What things do you think are important to look for in a new home? Make a list.

_____   _____

_____   _____

708   **Apartments for rent**

Westside Apartments

3 bdrm 2 ba furn apt New kit
$1000/mo Util incl Call mgr

555-1002 eves

Oxford Picture Dictionary pp. 50–51

🎧 **1.** Listen to the entire conversation between a manager and a woman looking for an apartment. Answer the questions with your class.

    a. What kind of apartment is the woman looking for?

    b. Is she going to move in?

🎧 **2.** Listen to each part of the conversation. Underline *True* or *False*.

a. The woman saw a vacancy sign.	True	False
b. The woman has children.	True	False
c. Some apartments have balconies.	True	False
d. There are six storage lockers.	True	False
e. Every apartment has an intercom.	True	False
f. The apartment is really nice.	True	False

🎧 **3.** Check (✔) the words you heard. Then listen again and check your answers.

☐ apartment complex	☐ landlord	☐ stairway	☐ second floor
☐ laundry room	☐ buzzers	☐ swimming pool	☐ washers
☐ recreation room	☐ peepholes	☐ dryers	☐ door chains

4. Write the words you checked in exercise 3 in alphabetical order.

_____   _____

_____   _____

_____

_____

_____

🎧 **1.** Listen to the entire conversation. Answer the questions with your class.

    a. What are the son and daughter doing?

    b. Why aren't they happy about the carpet?

🎧 **2.** Listen to each part of the conversation. Underline the words you hear.

> **a.** Put it here across from the (sofa / window).
>
> **b.** I'll put the (houseplant / throw pillows) on it later.
>
> **c.** I'll bring in the (TV / entertainment centre).
>
> **d.** Put the houseplant on the (coffee table / fireplace).
>
> **e.** Should I put the (end tables / lamp) by the sofa?
>
> **f.** When I get my new (carpet / drapes), it will be perfect.

🎧 **3.** Check (✓) the words you heard. Then listen again and check your answers.

> ☐ sofa   ☐ TV   ☐ houseplant   ☐ loveseat
>
> ☐ drapes   ☐ end tables   ☐ mantle   ☐ stereo system
>
> ☐ DVD player   ☐ entertainment centre   ☐ lamp   ☐ coffee table

4. List things in your living room.

_____   _____

_____   _____

                                 _____

                                 _____

                                 _____

Oxford Picture Dictionary p. 60

🎧 1. Listen to the entire conversation. Answer the questions with your class.

    a. What does the couple have to do?

    b. What does the man tell the woman not to do? Why?

🎧 2. Listen to each part of the conversation. Underline the words you hear.

> **a.** Don't forget to (vacuum / sweep) the floor first.
>
> **b.** I'll (recycle the newspapers / wash the dishes) and you can dry them.
>
> **c.** I'll tell them to (put away / wash) their toys.
>
> **d.** I'll just (polish / take out) these bags of garbage.

🎧 3. Check (✓) the words you heard. Then listen again and check your answers.

> ☐ clean the oven   ☐ dry the dishes   ☐ mop the floor   ☐ empty the trash
>
> ☐ vacuum the carpet   ☐ change the sheets   ☐ wash the windows   ☐ make the bed
>
> ☐ put away the toys   ☐ dust the furniture   ☐ wipe the counter   ☐ polish the furniture

4. List the housework that you enjoy doing and the housework you don't enjoy doing.

Enjoy	**Don't Enjoy**
_____	_____
_____	_____
_____	_____
_____	_____

Disc 1, Track 18

🎧 1. Listen to the entire conversation between a husband and a wife. Answer the questions with your class.

    a. What did the man find?

    b. How does the woman feel at first? How does she feel at the end of the conversation?

🎧 2. Listen to each part of the conversation. Underline the words you hear.

> **a.** Well, one of the bedroom windows is (broken / cracked).
>
> **b.** And the kitchen faucet is (leaking / dripping) a little bit.
>
> **c.** I think we'll need to call a (roofer / carpenter).
>
> **d.** Are there (mice / cockroaches)?

🎧 3. Check (✓) the words you heard. Then listen again and check your answers.

> ☐ broken   ☐ frozen   ☐ locksmith   ☐ dripping
>
> ☐ plumber   ☐ exterminator   ☐ stopped up   ☐ roofer
>
> ☐ rats   ☐ overflowing   ☐ leaking   ☐ termites

    4. Write the words you checked in exercise 3 in the chart.

Repair Person	Problem

Oxford Picture Dictionary p. 69

1. Listen to the entire conversation about two different salads. Answer the questions with your class.

   a. What's the difference between the two salads?

   b. Which salad would you like better?

2. Close your book. Listen to each part of the conversation. Underline the words you hear.

   a. a (head of lettuce / bag of lettuce)

   b. yellow (radishes / bell peppers)

   c. half a (zucchini / cucumber)

   d. purple (cabbage / beets)

   e. green (beans / onions)

   f. a (head of lettuce / bag of lettuce)

3. Check (✓) the words you heard. Then listen again and check your answers.

☐ head of lettuce	☐ cucumber	☐ onion	☐ bell peppers
☐ corn	☐ spinach	☐ radishes	☐ zucchini
☐ mushrooms	☐ potatoes	☐ carrots	☐ tomato

4. List your favourite salad vegetables and your favourite cooked vegetables.

Salad Vegetables	**Cooked Vegetables**
_____	_____
_____	_____
_____	_____
_____	_____

🎧 1. Listen to the entire conversation between the customer and the clerk. Answer the questions with your class.

    a. Why does the woman need a cake?

    b. Why is the customer confused?

🎧 2. Close your book. Listen to each part of the conversation. Underline the words you hear.

> **a.** I'm looking for the (sugar / cake).
>
> **b.** Oh, I also need (cookies / flour) and oil.
>
> **c.** And I need (eggs / ice cream).
>
> **d.** Maybe I should buy a (cake / cookies).
>
> **e.** Do you like (ice cream / cake)?
>
> **f.** Where are the (checkouts / customers)?

🎧 3. Check (✓) the words you heard. Then listen again and check your answers.

> ☐ cake ☐ bakery ☐ frozen foods ☐ baking products
> ☐ yogourt ☐ checkouts ☐ tuna ☐ aisle
> ☐ bagger ☐ dairy ☐ manager ☐ cashiers

4. Write the items you checked in exercise 3 in the chart.

Places in the Store	Food	People

Oxford Picture Dictionary p. 74

🎧 1. Listen to the entire conversation between a husband and a wife. Answer the questions with your class.

    a. Where is the man going? Why?

    b. How does he remember anything?

🎧 2. Close your book. Listen to each part of the conversation. Underline *True* or *False*.

a. He wants soda.	True	False
b. She wants strawberries.	True	False
c. She wants peanut butter.	True	False
d. They need cereal.	True	False
e. They have eggs.	True	False
f. She wants milk.	True	False

🎧 3. Check (✓) the items on the man's list. Then listen again and check your answers.

☐ two boxes of cereal	☐ a carton of eggs	☐ a jar of jam	☐ a loaf of bread
☐ two packages of cookies	☐ a bag of potatoes	☐ a bag of flour	☐ a bottle of water
☐ a container of yogourt	☐ a bottle of orange juice	☐ a can of beans	☐ a carton of milk

4. List foods and other items in your cabinet and refrigerator.

Cabinet	Refrigerator

🎧 1. Listen to the entire conversation. Answer the questions with your class.

    a. Why is Chef Zamora on the show?

    b. Is the show's host happy with what Chef Zamora makes?

🎧 2. Listen to each part of the conversation. Underline the words you hear.

> **a.** Would you like me to (grease / preheat) the oven?
>
> **b.** We're going to (sauté / peel) the onions and garlic.
>
> **c.** Now add in that cheese that I (boiled / grated) earlier.
>
> **d.** I'll probably just (microwave / steam) them; that's much faster.

🎧 3. Check (✓) the words you heard. Then listen again and check your answers.

> ☐ preheat   ☐ simmer   ☐ beat   ☐ microwave
>
> ☐ chill   ☐ spoon   ☐ bake   ☐ boil
>
> ☐ dice   ☐ slice   ☐ cut up   ☐ grate

    4. Write the words you checked in exercise 3 in alphabetical order.

    _____   _____

    _____   _____

    _____

    _____

    _____

    _____

A Coffee Shop Menu
LISTENING EXERCISES

Oxford Picture Dictionary pp. 80–81

🎧 1. Look at the menu on pages 80 and 81 in the OPD. Listen to the entire conversation between the server and the customer. Answer the questions with your class.

    a. Does the man have the spaghetti dinner? Why or why not?

    b. What is the customer's final order?

🎧 2. Close your book. Listen to each part of the conversation. Underline *True* or *False*.

a. He wants a cup of coffee.	True	False
b. He is eating dinner.	True	False
c. He wants tea.	True	False
d. He eats a club sandwich.	True	False

🎧 3. Check (✓) the words you heard. Then listen again and check your answers.

☐ cheesecake	☐ spinach salad	☐ milk	☐ club sandwich
☐ ranch dressing	☐ grilled cheese sandwich	☐ cream	☐ Italian dressing
☐ layer cake	☐ chef's salad	☐ tea	☐ soup

4. Write the foods you checked in exercise 3 in the chart.

Lunch	
Salad Dressings	
Desserts	
Beverages	

     Disc 1, Track 24

🎧 **1.** Look at pages 88 and 89 in the OPD. Listen to the entire conversation. Point to the people. Then answer the questions with your class.

    a. What are the women doing in the hotel lobby?

    b. Does the woman prefer the evening gown or the cocktail dress?

    c. How do they know the two people are working?

🎧 **2.** Close your book. Listen to each part of the conversation. Underline *True* or *False*.

a. They see a little girl in overalls.	True	False
b. They like the evening dress.	True	False
c. They think the bellhop is hot in his uniform.	True	False
d. They like the man's tie.	True	False

🎧 **3.** Check (✓) the words you heard. Then listen again and check your answers.

☐ overalls	☐ cocktail dress	☐ tank top	☐ maternity dress
☐ clutch bag	☐ business suits	☐ briefcase	☐ shorts
☐ tuxedo	☐ evening gown	☐ capris	☐ tie

4. Look at your classmates. List the clothing you see people wearing.

Women	Men	Both

Oxford Picture Dictionary pp. 94–95

🎧 1. Listen to the entire conversation between Tom and his friend at the store. Answer the questions with your class.

    a. What is Tom looking for?

    b. What will he get his wife?

🎧 2. Listen to each part of the conversation. Underline the words you hear.

> **a.** I'm just looking at the (jewellery / watches).
>
> **b.** Well, how about those plastic (belt buckles / beads)?
>
> **c.** Maybe I'll get her some (earrings / bracelets).
>
> **d.** I don't like (hats / belts).
>
> **e.** I'm going to look at the (shoes / purses).
>
> **f.** These (watches / wallets) are nice.

🎧 3. Check (✓) the words you heard. Then listen again and check your answers.

> ☐ necklace   ☐ bracelets   ☐ wallets   ☐ string of pearls
>
> ☐ clip-on earrings   ☐ watches   ☐ belts   ☐ scarves
>
> ☐ display case   ☐ pierced earrings   ☐ backpack   ☐ locket

4. Write the words you checked in exercise 3 in the chart.

Jewellery	Other Accessories

🎧 **1.** Listen to the entire conversation between a mother and her son. Answer the questions with your class.

    a. Who is doing the laundry?

    b. What does Billy need to do first?

    c. Why must Billy take out the red T-shirt?

🎧 **2.** Listen to each part of the conversation. Underline the words you hear.

---

    a. Do you want to wear (clean / dirty) clothes?

    b. First, you need to (dry / sort) the clothes.

    c. Now load the (dryer / washer).

    d. Now you have to put the clothes in the (washer / dryer).

    e. You need to (iron / unload) the clothes.

    f. The (clothesline / ironing board) is right there.

🎧 **3.** Check (✓) the words you heard. Then listen again and check your answers.

☐ laundry	☐ wet	☐ fold	☐ bleach
☐ dryer	☐ wrinkled	☐ laundry detergent	☐ dryer sheet
☐ iron	☐ hanger	☐ clothespin	

---

4. Write the words you checked in exercise 3 in alphabetical order.

Oxford Picture Dictionary pp. 108–109

🎧 1. Listen to the woman and her daughter in the drugstore. Answer the questions with your class.

    a. What does the girl want?

    b. Which items won't the mother buy for her daughter?

🎧 2. Listen to each part of the conversation. Underline the words you hear.

---

    a. We need (shampoo / sunscreen).

    b. We don't need (cologne / conditioner).

    c. Look at this (blow dryer / bath powder).

    d. Let's get some (toothbrushes / toothpaste).

    e. Let's get some (shavers / razors).

    f. Look, there's the (mouthwash / makeup).

🎧 3. Check (✔) the words you heard. Then listen again and check your answers.

☐ shampoo	☐ mouthwash	☐ shaving cream	☐ wash
☐ toothpaste	☐ sunscreen	☐ shower gel	☐ razors
☐ makeup	☐ blow dryer	☐ deodorant	☐ lipstick

---

4. Write the words you checked in exercise 3 in alphabetical order.

_____   _____

_____   _____

_____

_____

_____

_____

Oxford Picture Dictionary p. 110

🎧 **1.** Mandy is a receptionist at a doctor's office. Listen to her telephone conversations. Answer the questions with your class.

    a. Which caller is coming in first?

    b. Which caller is not coming in?

🎧 **2.** Listen to each conversation. Underline *True* or *False*.

a. Mr. Han's appointment is at 2:00.	True	False
b. Annie Jackson will be there in 15 minutes.	True	False
c. The third man doesn't say his name.	True	False
d. Brian needs to see the doctor.	True	False

🎧 **3.** Check (✓) the words you heard. Then listen again and check your answers.

☐ headache	☐ stomach ache	☐ dizzy	☐ earache
☐ sort throat	☐ backache	☐ temperature	☐ cough
☐ insect bite	☐ rash	☐ chills	☐ swollen

4. Write the words you checked in exercise 3 in alphabetical order.

_____   _____

_____   _____

    _____

    _____

    _____

    _____

Oxford Picture Dictionary pp. 112–113

🎧 **1.** Listen to the conversations at the pharmacy. Answer the questions with your class.

    a. What will the customer take for back pain?

    b. What things does the pharmacist tell customers not to do?

🎧 **2.** Listen to each conversation. Underline *True* or *False*.

a. Mr. Randall is dropping off a prescription.	True	False
b. Mr. Randall has back pain.	True	False
c. He should take one pill every four hours.	True	False
d. This customer is looking for capsules.	True	False

🎧 **3.** Check (✓) the words you heard. Then listen again and check your answers.

☐ prescription label	☐ dosage	☐ inhaler	☐ pain reliever
☐ over-the-counter medication	☐ eye drops	☐ antacid	☐ finish
☐ capsules	☐ take	☐ pills	☐ syrups

4. Write the words you checked in exercise 3 in alphabetical order.

_____   _____

_____   _____

_____

_____

_____

R DUGGEN DRUGS
123 Main Street
#639180 9/1/10
Brian Prescod
2 capsules
2 times a day
Tetracycline
Qty. 20
Dr. M. Burns
Exp. 3/3/11
DEA# BG4365183
No refills
DO NOT TAKE WITH DAIRY PRODUCTS

1. Listen to the conversations. Answer the questions with your class.

   a. What does Dr. Ohja tell the second patient to do?

   b. Which patient does Dr. Ohja send to the hospital?

2. Listen to each part of the conversation. Underline the words you hear.

   a. If you stay fit and (drink fluids / eat a healthy diet), you should have more energy.

   b. Have you been having any (hearing loss / vision problems)?

   c. Didn't you (get immunized / have regular checkups) before you left?

   d. I can recommend a (support group / therapist) for you.

3. Check (✓) the words you heard. Then listen again and check your answers.

   ☐ seek medical attention   ☐ hearing loss   ☐ depression   ☐ support group
   ☐ follow medical advice   ☐ get bed rest   ☐ stay fit   ☐ drink fluids
   ☐ vision problems   ☐ optometrist   ☐ take medicine ☐ audiologist

4. Write the words you checked in exercise 3 in alphabetical order.

   _____   _____

   _____   _____

          _____

                               _____

                               _____

Oxford Picture Dictionary p. 118

🎧 **1.** Listen to the entire conversation. Answer the questions with your class.

    a. Why does the patient visit Dr. Willis?

    b. Why does Dr. Willis decide to do more tests?

🎧 **2.** Listen to each part of the conversation. Underline the words you hear.

> **a.** I see you've filled out your (health history form / blood pressure gauge).
>
> **b.** Please have a seat on the (stethoscope / examination table).
>
> **c.** I'm going to (examine / listen to) your eyes, ears, and throat.
>
> **d.** Yes, I'm going to use this (syringe / thermometer) to draw some of your blood.
>
> **e.** Check with my (nurse / receptionist).

🎧 **3.** Check (✓) the words you heard. Then listen again and check your answers.

> ☐ syringe   ☐ examination table   ☐ receptionist   ☐ nurse
>
> ☐ patient   ☐ blood pressure gauge   ☐ draw blood   ☐ doctor
>
> ☐ health card   ☐ check blood pressure   ☐ thermometer   ☐ appointment

4. Write the words you checked in exercise 3 in alphabetical order.

Oxford Picture Dictionary pp. 120–121

🎧 **1.** Listen to the conversations at the hospital. Answer the questions with your class.

    a. Why is Mrs. Morales at the hospital?

    b. When can Mrs. Morales eat?

🎧 **2.** Listen to each part of the conversation. Underline the hospital employees that Mrs. Morales sees.

> **a.** admissions clerk / doctor and nurse / orderly
>
> **b.** nursing assistant / nurse
>
> **c.** cardiologist / nurse
>
> **d.** phlebotomist / surgeon
>
> **e.** surgeon / anesthesiologist

🎧 **3.** Check (✓) the words you heard. Then listen again and check your answers.

> ☐ patient   ☐ bed control   ☐ phlebotomist   ☐ nursing assistant
>
> ☐ call button   ☐ surgical gloves   ☐ dietician   ☐ bedpan
>
> ☐ blood test   ☐ hospital gown   ☐ volunteer   ☐ anesthesiologist

4. Write the words you checked in exercise 3 in the chart.

People in the Hospital	Things in the Hospital

Oxford Picture Dictionary pp. 126–127

🎧 **1.** Listen to the entire conversation. Answer the questions with your class.

    a. Why is the man asking for directions?

    b. Which places does he ask for directions to?

🎧 **2.** Listen to each part of the conversation. Underline the words you hear.

    a. It's across the street from the (synagogue / college).

    b. Do you know how to get to the (gym / furniture store)?

    c. Is that on the same street as the (mosque / bakery)?

    d. It's on Maple Street, between the bakery and the (school / church).

    e. Here's the (coffee shop / shopping mall).

🎧 **3.** Check (✓) the words you heard. Then listen again and check your answers.

☐ factory	☐ construction site	☐ coffee shop	☐ bakery
☐ garbage truck	☐ furniture store	☐ college	☐ skyscraper
☐ motel	☐ convention centre	☐ gym	☐ theatre

4. Look at pages 126 and 127 in the OPD. Make a list of the buildings you usually pass on your way to school.

_____   _____

_____   _____

_____

_____   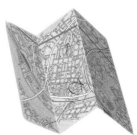

_____

_____

Oxford Picture Dictionary pp. 128–129

🎧 1. Look at pages 128 and 129 in the OPD. Listen to the phone call between two friends. Answer the question with your class.

Where are they going to meet?

🎧 2. Close your book. Listen to each part of the conversation. Underline the words you hear.

> **a.** The (childcare centre / convenience store) opens at 8:00.
>
> **b.** What time does the (restaurant / laundromat) open?
>
> **c.** The (pharmacy / video store) opens at 9:00.
>
> **d.** It's near the (laundromat / barbershop).
>
> **e.** There's a (bus stop / newsstand) across from Burger Queen.
>
> **f.** It's across from the (pharmacy / doughnut shop).

🎧 3. Check (✔) the words you heard. Then listen again and check your answers.

> ☐ childcare centre   ☐ bus   ☐ doughnut shop   ☐ dry cleaners
>
> ☐ convenience store ☐ sidewalk   ☐ laundromat   ☐ traffic light
>
> ☐ corner   ☐ parking space ☐ mailbox   ☐ parking meter

4. Write the words you checked in exercise 3 in alphabetical order.

_____ _____

_____ _____

_____

_____

_____

_____

Oxford Picture Dictionary p. 132

🎧 1. Listen to the entire conversation. Answer the questions with your class.

    a. Why is the woman at the bank?

    b. What does the account manager give to the woman right away?

    c. What is he going to send to her in a few weeks?

🎧 2. Listen to each part of the conversation. Underline the words you hear.

> **a.** I'm the (account manager / customer) here, so I can help you open your account.
>
> **b.** No, you'll just have to carry your (deposit slip / ATM card) and remember your PIN.
>
> **c.** Finally, would you like to rent a (chequebook / safety deposit box)?
>
> **d.** You'll just need to fill out a (cheque / deposit slip).
>
> **e.** If you'd like, you can (bank online / withdraw cash) instead.

🎧 3. Check (✓) the words you heard. Then listen again and check your answers.

> ☐ savings account number   ☐ account manager   ☐ teller   ☐ vault
>
> ☐ security guard   ☐ deposit   ☐ ATM card   ☐ balance
>
> ☐ safety deposit box   ☐ chequebook   ☐ bank online   ☐ customer

    4. Write the words you checked in exercise 3 in alphabetical order.

    _____   _____

    _____   _____

    _____   _____

    _____   _____

🎧 **1.** Listen to the library information line. Listen to all the messages. Answer the questions with your class.

    a. What is the name of the library?

    b. When is the library open?

🎧 **2.** Listen to each message. Underline *True* or *False*.

a. For a library card, you need a photo ID.	True False
b. You can use the online catalogue at home.	True False
c. You can keep a book for four weeks.	True False
d. You can put DVDs in the box.	True False

🎧 **3.** Check (✓) the words you heard. Then listen again and check your answers.

☐ get	☐ audiobooks	☐ check out	☐ look for
☐ novels	☐ self-checkout	☐ magazines	☐ DVDs
☐ newspapers	☐ picture books	☐ periodicals	☐ return

4. Write the words you checked in exercise 3 in alphabetical order.

_____   _____

_____   _____

                                                  _____

TOMMY DOUGLAS:
The Life of a
Great Canadian
by Anna Scott

TRUDEAU PUBLIC LIBRARY
CENTRAL BRANCH

CHECK OUT DATE: APRIL 15
DUE DATE: MAY 06

TOMMY DOUGLAS:
THE LIFE OF A
GREAT CANADIAN

LATE FINE: $.10 A DAY

TOTAL ITEMS: 1

Oxford Picture Dictionary pp. 136–137

🎧 1. Look at pages 136 and 137 in the OPD. Listen to the conversations between the licensing clerk and the customers. Answer the questions with your class.

   a. How many customers are there?

   b. What is the second customer's problem?

🎧 2. Close your book. Listen to each conversation. Underline the words you hear.

> **a.** I'm ready to take my (driving / written) test.
>
> **b.** I want to get my driver's (licence / permit).
>
> **c.** I'd like to get a (beginner's permit / licence plate).
>
> **d.** What kind of (photo / identification) do you need?

🎧 3. Check (✓) the words you heard. Then listen again and check your answers.

> ☐ beginner's permit   ☐ signature   ☐ show   ☐ written test
>
> ☐ registration stickers   ☐ vision exam   ☐ driving test   ☐ pay
>
> ☐ driver's licence number   ☐ proof of insurance   ☐ window   ☐ licence plate

4. Write the words you checked in exercise 3 in alphabetical order.

_____ _____

_____ _____

_____

_____

_____

🎧 **1.** Listen to the entire conversation. Answer the questions with your class.

    a. What job does the woman have?

    b. What other jobs has she had in the past?

🎧 **2.** Listen to each part of the conversation. Underline the words you hear.

---

    a. Earlier today, our new (premier / prime minister) was sworn in.

    b. I worked in the (Senate / House of Commons) for almost ten years.

    c. And what did you do before becoming a (member of parliament / city councillor)?

    d. My (opponents / election results) in the riding were very experienced and were excellent speakers.

    e. I don't know, maybe I'll become a (chief justice / senator)!

🎧 **3.** Check (✔) the words you heard. Then listen again and check your answers.

☐ premier	☐ city council	☐ member of parliament	☐ run for office
☐ serve	☐ cabinet	☐ Parliament of Canada	☐ Governor General
☐ judges	☐ senator	☐ political campaign	☐ opponents

---

4. Write the words you checked in exercise 3 in alphabetical order.

_____

_____

_____

_____

_____

_____

Oxford Picture Dictionary p. 140

🎧 1. Listen to the entire conversation. Answer the questions with your class.

    a. What is Mustafa doing today?

    b. Why does he want to do this?

🎧 2. Listen to each part of the conversation. Underline the words you hear.

> **a.** I'm on my way to (take my citizenship test / eliminate discrimination and injustice).
>
> **b.** You must (be at least 18 years old / vote in elections).
>
> **c.** In Canada, I can use my writing to express my opinions because I have the freedom of (thought, belief, opinion, and expression / conscience and religion).
>
> **d.** We were able to do that because of our right to (freedom of association / peaceful assembly).
>
> **e.** For example, they should obey the country's laws and (express opinions freely while respecting the rights and freedoms of others / help others in their communities).
>
> **f.** Once I'm a citizen, it will also be my responsibility to (vote in elections / take a citizenship test).

🎧 3. Check (✔) the words you heard. Then listen again and check your answers.

> | | | |
> |---|---|---|
> | ☐ freedom of association | ☐ peaceful assembly | ☐ take a citizenship test |
> | ☐ care for and protect our heritage and environment | ☐ live in Canada for 3 of the last 4 years | ☐ eliminate discrimination and prejudice |
> | ☐ freedom of conscience and religion | ☐ help others in the community | ☐ freedom of thought, belief, opinion, and expression |
> | ☐ vote in elections | ☐ be 18 or older | ☐ obey Canada's laws |

4. Look at the top of page 140 in the OPD. Choose one of the responsibilities listed and explain why it is important.

_____

_____

_____

_____

Oxford Picture Dictionary p. 143

1. Listen to the entire conversation. Answer the questions with your class.

    a. Why does Sabrina take Paula's purse?

    b. What advice does Paula give to Sabrina?

2. Listen to each part of the conversation. Underline the words you hear.

> **a.** You didn't (conceal / lock) your apartment door.
>
> **b.** You should (protect your purse / report a suspicious package) by keeping it close to your body.
>
> **c.** You should always (walk with a friend / shop on secure websites) in the evening so you're not alone.
>
> **d.** We should stay on this street—it's (a neighbourhood watch / well-lit).
>
> **e.** Always (conceal / lock) your PIN when you're at the ATM.

3. Check (✓) the words you heard. Then listen again and check your answers.

> ☐ walk with a friend   ☐ lock your doors   ☐ conceal your PIN
>
> ☐ don't open your door to strangers   ☐ be aware of your surroundings   ☐ join a neighbourhood watch
>
> ☐ protect your purse or wallet   ☐ report suspicious packages   ☐ report crimes to the police
>
> ☐ shop on secure websites   ☐ stay on well-lit streets   ☐ don't drink and drive

4. Look at the safety tips on page 143 in the OPD. Write two additional tips of your own.

_____

_____

_____

_____

_____

Oxford Picture Dictionary pp. 146–147

🎧 1. Listen to the guest speaker talk to the class. Listen to the entire talk. Answer the questions with your class.

    a. What committee is Ms. Thomas from?

    b. What is she talking about?

🎧 2. Listen to each part of the talk. Underline the words you hear.

    a. We need to (plan / take cover) for an emergency.

    b. You need (packaged food / canned food).

    c. You should have (blankets / matches).

    d. Don't forget the extra (canned food / batteries).

    e. What about a (flashlight / first aid kit)?

    f. Include (cash and coins / copies of ID and credit cards).

🎧 3. Check (✔) the words you heard. Then listen again and check your answers.

☐ plan	☐ copies of important papers	☐ first aid kit	☐ make
☐ seek	☐ moist towelettes	☐ matches	☐ evacuate
☐ flashlight	☐ copies of ID and credit cards	☐ bottled water	☐ can opener

4. Write the words you checked in exercise 3 in alphabetical order.

_____   _____

_____   _____

_____

_____

_____

🎧 **1.** Look at page 152 in the OPD. Listen to the conversations. Point to the locations as you listen.

🎧 **2.** Close your book. Listen to each conversation. Underline the locations.

> **a.** train station / bus stop
>
> **b.** bus / subway station
>
> **c.** train station / bus stop
>
> **d.** bus / taxi
>
> **e.** train / bus

🎧 **3.** Check (✓) the words you heard. Then listen again and check your answers.

☐ ticket	☐ vending machine	☐ meter	☐ platform
☐ turnstile	☐ taxi licence	☐ tokens	☐ town car
☐ shuttle	☐ subway car	☐ schedule	☐ rider

4. What types of public transportation do you use regularly?

_____

_____

_____

_____

_____

Oxford Picture Dictionary p. 155

🎧 **1.** Look at the map at the bottom left of page 155 in the OPD. Listen to the conversations. Point to the streets as you listen.

🎧 **B.** Close your book. Listen to each conversation. Underline *True* or *False*.

> **a.** Tara is at 19th Street East and Broadway Avenue. True False
>
> **b.** Sal is near Friendship Park. True False
>
> **c.** Mary is at 3rd Avenue North and 25th Street East. True False
>
> **d.** Edgar is on 22nd Street West near Leif Erickson Park. True False
>
> **e.** Jin is on Avenue H South near Victoria Park. True False

🎧 **3.** Listen again. Check (✓) the words you heard.

> ☐ go ☐ GPS ☐ turn right ☐ stop
>
> ☐ river ☐ west ☐ highway ☐ go straight
>
> ☐ key ☐ east ☐ railroad track ☐ Internet map

4. Look at the map at the bottom left of page 155 in the OPD. Read the directions. Answer the question.

a. Start at 19th Street West and Avenue H South.

b. Go north on Avenue H South to 22nd Street West and turn right.

c. Go east on 22nd Street West.

d. Go past Idylwyld Drive and 1st Avenue.

Where are you? _____

_____

_____

Oxford Picture Dictionary pp. 160–161

🎧 **1.** Listen to the entire conversation. Answer the questions with your class.

    a. How does Scott know that the flight will be on time?

    b. Why does Scott's father put Scott's bag in the overhead compartment?

🎧 **2.** Listen to each part of the conversation. Underline the words you hear.

> **a.** Do you see any (bins / porters)?
>
> **b.** It'll be faster if we (go through security / check in electronically).
>
> **c.** There's the (boarding area / flight attendant) for our gate.
>
> **d.** Do you have your (boarding pass / check-in kiosk)?
>
> **e.** Hey, they just called us to (board the plane / claim our baggage).
>
> **f.** Be sure to (find your seat / fasten your seatbelt).

🎧 **3.** Check (✓) the words you heard. Then listen again and check your answers.

> ☐ gate   ☐ customs officer   ☐ upright seat   ☐ check-in kiosk
>
> ☐ board the plane   ☐ pilot   ☐ flight attendant   ☐ luggage
>
> ☐ turbulence   ☐ oxygen mask   ☐ ticket agent   ☐ passenger

4. Write the words you checked in exercise 3 in alphabetical order.

    _____   _____

    _____   _____

    _____

    _____

    _____

    _____

Oxford Picture Dictionary p. 171

🎧 1. Listen to the entire conversation. Answer the question with your class.

   What tasks does Ms Chang ask Donald to do?

🎧 2. Listen to each part of the conversation. Underline the words you hear.

> **a.** First, I'll need you to (transcribe the notes / scan these documents).
>
> **b.** Can you (leave a message / schedule a meeting) with Mr. Goldstein so I can discuss my notes with him?
>
> **c.** Please (greet / make) twenty copies of these sales reports and staple them.
>
> **d.** Should I (transfer the call / fax a document) to you?
>
> **e.** Did Mr. Goldstein (enter data / leave a message) for me?

🎧 3. Check (✓) the words you heard. Then listen again and check your answers.

> ☐ check messages   ☐ collate papers   ☐ staple   ☐ transcribe
>
> ☐ print   ☐ schedule a meeting   ☐ type a letter   ☐ fax
>
> ☐ organize   ☐ take dictation   ☐ transfer   ☐ check messages

4. Write the words you checked in exercise 3 in alphabetical order.

_____   _____

_____   _____

_____

_____

_____

1. Look at page 172 in the OPD. Listen to the conversations at the Job Resource Centre. Answer the questions with your class.

   a. What does the man want?

   b. How does Mrs. Alvarez feel at the end?

2. Listen to each conversation. Underline the words you hear.

   a. Welcome to the (Resource / Career) Centre.

   b. I'm interested in finding a new (career / job).

   c. After that, you can complete the (skill / interest) inventory.

   d. Do you offer (jobs / training) here?

   e. Yes, we have a (recruiter / counsellor).

3. Check (✔) the words you heard. Then listen again and check your answers.

   ☐ career counsellor   ☐ online course   ☐ entry-level job   ☐ job fairs

   ☐ interest inventory   ☐ promotion   ☐ internships   ☐ skill inventory

   ☐ vocational training   ☐ recruiters   ☐ on-the-job training   ☐ resource centre

4. What jobs would you like to do? Make a list.

_____   _____

_____   _____

_____   _____

Oxford Picture Dictionary p. 174

🎧 **1.** Look at page 174 in the OPD. Listen to the radio show. Answer the questions with your class.

    a. What is Jill Thurman giving advice about?

    b. What should you not do in an interview?

🎧 **2.** Listen to each part of the show. Underline the suggestions you hear.

> **a.** First, (be neat / be on time / shake hands).
>
> **b.** Second, (dress appropriately / listen carefully / thank the interviewer).
>
> **c.** Third, (turn off your cellphone / make eye contact / be neat).
>
> **d.** And fourth, (bring your resume and ID / ask questions / shake hands).

🎧 **3.** Underline *True* or *False*. Then listen again and check your answers.

    a. If you are late for the interview, the employer will think you'll be late for work.   True   False

    b. It's OK to dress casually for some job interviews.   True   False

    c. If you don't look at an interviewer, he or she will think you are respectful.   True   False

    d. "Do you offer training?" is a good question.   True   False

4. Cross out the statements that are not advice for a job interview.

Be neat.	Shake hands.	Give short answers.
Be late.	Ask about vacations.	Turn off your cellphone.

Oxford Picture Dictionary pp. 180–181

🎧 **1.** Look at page 181 in the OPD. Listen to the entire conversation. Answer the questions with your class.

    a. What is the woman going to paint?

    _____

    b. What colour does she like?

    _____

🎧 **2.** Close your dictionary. Listen to each part of the conversation. Underline the supplies you hear.

    a. You'll need a (paint roller / spray gun).

    b. The (tape measures / drop cloths) are on that wall.

    c. This is a good (scraper / wire stripper).

    d. The (wood stain / paint) is right here.

🎧 **3.** Check (✓) the words you heard. Then listen again and check your answers.

☐ paint roller	☐ drop cloths	☐ scraper	☐ paint tray
☐ masking tape	☐ sandpaper	☐ hammer	☐ outlet covers
☐ nail	☐ pipe	☐ screw	☐ wood stain

4. Write short answers.

    a. What colour is your living room? _____

    b. Do you like to paint? _____

    c. Do you like to fix things? _____

Oxford Picture Dictionary pp. 182–183

🎧 **1.** Look at the office on page 182 in the OPD. Listen to the conversations. Answer the questions with your class.

    a. How many phone calls does the receptionist get?

    b. Where is Mrs. Tam?

    c. What is the office manager's problem?

🎧 **2.** Close your dictionary. Listen to each section. Underline the job titles you hear.

> **a.** Well, how about her (receptionist / administrative assistant)?
>
> **b.** I'd like to speak to the (executive / office manager).
>
> **c.** And please find the (computer technician / clerk) for me.
>
> **d.** Do you mean Roland, the (office manager / file clerk)?

🎧 **3.** Check (✓) the words you heard. Then listen again and check your answers.

> ☐ receptionist   ☐ office manager   ☐ clerk   ☐ desk
>
> ☐ supply cabinet   ☐ conference room   ☐ file cabinet   ☐ computer
>
> ☐ reception area   ☐ presentation   ☐ fax machine   ☐ executives

4. Number these sentences in the correct order.

    _____ I'm sorry. Mr. White isn't in his office. May I take a message?

    _____ May I speak to Mr. White, please?

    _____ Oh, that's OK. I'll call back this afternoon.

    _____ Blue Steel Corporation. How can I help you?

🎧 **1.** Look at page 197 in the OPD. Listen to the entire conversation between the mother and the daughter. Answer the questions with your class.

    a. What is the woman trying to find?

    b. What was the girl using the computer for?

🎧 **2.** Close your dictionary. Listen to each part of the conversation. Underline the correct word.

> **a.** I think the (URL / search engine) is www.TV101.ca.
>
> **b.** You have to put your (cursor / pointer) over the box.
>
> **c.** Type your (user name / address) and your password.
>
> **d.** Don't forget to (type / click) a subject.
>
> **e.** Just click the (video / back) button.

🎧 **3.** Check (✓) the words you heard. Then listen again and check your answers.

> ☐ video   ☐ pop-up ad   ☐ back button   ☐ type
>
> ☐ send   ☐ address   ☐ search box   ☐ cursor
>
> ☐ menu bar   ☐ search engine   ☐ scroll bar   ☐ forward button

4. What do you use the Internet for? Check (✓) the items.

     ☐ shopping   ☐ videos   ☐ games

     ☐ news   ☐ studying   ☐ chat

     ☐ email   ☐ music

Oxford Picture Dictionary p. 198

🎧 1. Look at page 198 in the OPD. Listen to the teacher and the students. Answer the questions with your class.

    a. What kind of class is this?

    b. Do the students know the answers?

🎧 2. Close your dictionary. Listen to each part of the conversation. Underline the correct word.

> **a.** There were four (provinces / settlers).
>
> **b.** Those people are called the (Inuit / Fathers of Confederation).
>
> **c.** Is it the (North American Free Trade Agreement / British North America Act)?
>
> **d.** The British North America Act was created by the (Fathers of Confederation / settlers).
>
> **e.** Sir John A. Macdonald was the (First Nations / first prime minister).

🎧 3. Check (✓) the words you heard. Then listen again and check your answers.

> ☐ First Nations ☐ settlers ☐ Halifax explosion ☐ Inuit
> ☐ Great Depression ☐ Constitution Act ☐ British North America Act ☐ World War II
> ☐ first prime minister ☐ provinces ☐ Fathers of Confederation ☐ World War I

4. Order these events from oldest to most recent. (1 = the oldest)

_____ Battle of the Plains of Abraham

_____ Canada becomes officially bilingual (English and French)

_____ Women get the right to vote

_____ Confederation: Canada is formed

_____ Canada participates in World War I

Oxford Picture Dictionary pp. 200–201

🎧 **1.** Look at pages 200 and 201 in the OPD. Listen to Gina talk about her trip. As you listen, point to the states you hear.

🎧 **2.** Close your book. Listen to each part of the conversation. Underline the correct place.

> **a.** We drove to (Baffin Island / Prince Edward Island) and saw the Anne of Green Gables farmhouse.
>
> **b.** Then we drove west to (Vancouver / Calgary).
>
> **c.** After that we went through (Québec / Ontario) again, and we stayed in Québec City.
>
> **d.** Maybe we'll go to (the United States / Mexico).

🎧 **3.** Check (✓) the words you heard. Then listen again and check your answers.

> ☐ the Prairie Provinces ☐ the North ☐ Central America ☐ Ontario
>
> ☐ the Atantic provinces ☐ east ☐ the West Coast ☐ Manitoba
>
> ☐ the Pacific Northwest ☐ southeast ☐ the Pacific ☐ Nova Scotia

4. Check the Canadian provinces.

☐ Ontario   ☐ Regina   ☐ Winnipeg

☐ Saskatchewan   ☐ Toronto   ☐ Québec

☐ Manitoba

Oxford Picture Dictionary pp. 218–219

🎧 1. Look at pages 218 and 219 in the OPD. Listen to the teacher and the students. Answer the questions with your class.

   a. What's the problem with oil?

   b. What's another big problem?

🎧 2. Close your book. Listen to each part of the conversation. Underline the correct word.

> **a.** We use (oil / coal) for most of our energy needs.
>
> **b.** We can save energy by turning (on / off) lights.
>
> **c.** We can (recycle / reduce) bottles, cans, paper, and plastic.
>
> **d.** Don't (carpool / litter).

🎧 3. Check (✓) the words you heard. Then listen again and check your answers.

> ☐ save   ☐ reduce   ☐ smog   ☐ energy
>
> ☐ compost   ☐ reuse   ☐ use   ☐ pollution
>
> ☐ litter   ☐ wind power   ☐ buy   ☐ nuclear energy

4. Check the ways that you save energy.

   ☐ I recycle.   ☐ I carpool.

   ☐ I save water.   ☐ I turn off lights.

   ☐ I reduce trash.

🎧 1. Look at page 224 in the OPD. Listen to the little girl and her father. Answer the questions with your class.

    a. How does the girl feel at the park?

    b. What does she want to do?

    c. How does the father feel?

🎧 2. Close your book. Listen to each part of the conversation. Underline the correct word.

> **a.** I want to go on the (swings / slide).
>
> **b.** I want to climb the (bars / slide).
>
> **c.** Did you bring the (jump rope / wagon)?
>
> **d.** I want to go in the (sandbox / water fountain).
>
> **e.** Can I get a (tricycle / skateboard)?

🎧 3. Check (✓) the words you heard. Then listen again and check your answers.

> ☐ tricycle   ☐ bench   ☐ tennis court   ☐ playground
> ☐ jump rope   ☐ water fountain   ☐ push   ☐ pull
> ☐ have a picnic   ☐ climb   ☐ seesaw   ☐ bike

4. Check (✓) the things you like to do at the park.

    ☐ sit on the bench   ☐ ride a bicycle

    ☐ have a picnic   ☐ walk

    ☐ take my children to the playground